THE
REBEL
PUBLISHING
HOUSE

Editors:	Swami Yoga Pratap Bharati, Ma Aseema Bharti, Ma Yoga Sudha
Design:	Swami Nityaprem
Typesetting:	Ma Kamaal & Ma Prem Shunyo
Production:	Ma Deva Harito
Photography:	Osho Photo Services
Endpapers:	Swami Harisharan
Printing:	Thomson Press (India)

Published by The Rebel Publishing House Pvt. Ltd.,
50 Koregaon Park, 411001 Pune, India

ISBN 81 7261 071 8

THE PATH OF MEDITATION

Spontaneous talks given by Osho
to disciples and friends
at a meditation camp in
Mahabaleshwar, India

OSHO

In Loving Gratitude to Osho
Swami Dharma Chaitanya

THE PATH OF MEDITATION

A STEP BY STEP GUIDE TO MEDITATION

Contents

Introduction

*f*UNNILY enough, although I am something of a "book-worm," (as a child I often staggered home from the local lending library carrying eight to ten books – a week's supply in my school satchel, borrowed on my own and my sister's tickets) I have never been a great reader of Osho's books. I love listening to his discourse tapes; the sound of his voice and the famous gaps of silence between the words hold me spellbound. This for me has always been preferable to the written word, where something seemed to be lacking.

That was until, working in English Publications at Osho Commune International, I was asked to proofread the book you are holding in your hand. As I read, I began to feel that inner connection to Osho's words as if he was speaking and I was relaxing into those words here and now. The very first sentence, *I would like to welcome you, because you have a longing for the divine,* brought tears to my eyes.

If you too have this longing for the divine, *The Path of Meditation* is the book for you. These nine talks (or I'd rather describe them as 'conversations'), held at a small gathering in Mahabaleshwar, have that feel of intimacy which can only exist between a Master and disciple. Osho is present in every chapter, in every word and in every silence between the words – yes, you can really 'hear' them!

Each chapter deals with a different aspect of meditation: its foundation, its function on the spiritual journey of purifying the body, mind and emotions; its essential nature and how to integrate it into our everyday lives. And at the end of each chapter Osho leads the gathering into what he calls a 'resolution': "I will experience silence, I will experience meditation," while doing a particularly intense breathing technique.

I was living this book, not only reading it, as I joined Osho in the guided meditations and I experimented with this powerful resolution that he suggests.

As we reach the end of the book and leave the hills and the meditation camp behind I feel I am returning from a journey, no longer the same as I began it, but richer in both understanding and inner silence.

Ma Divyam Sonar

THE PATH OF MEDITATION

the foundation of meditation

Chapter 1

My Beloved Ones,

*f*IRST, I WOULD like to welcome you, because you have a longing for the divine; because you desire to rise above ordinary life towards the life of a seeker and because, despite your worldly desires, you have a thirst for truth.

The people who have felt the thirst for truth are fortunate; out of the millions of people who are born, only a few ever feel the longing for truth. To know truth is a great blessing – but even to have the longing for it is as great a blessing. Even if you don't attain it that is okay, but to never have experienced the thirst at all would be a great misfortune.

I would like to say that it is not important to know truth. What is important is that you have the longing for it, that you make every effort towards experiencing it, that you work hard for it and yearn for it, and that you are determined and do everything you can possibly do towards this end. If in spite of this you don't attain it that does not matter. But never to have experienced this thirst at all – that would be the greatest tragedy.

I would also like to say that to know truth is not as important as to have an authentic yearning for it. That yearning is a joy in itself. If the desire is for something insignificant, there will be no joy even if you get it; but if you long for the significant, the ultimate and you don't get it, then you will be filled with joy even if you don't get it. I repeat: if you desire a

2

small thing and you get it, you will still not be as happy as when you long for the ultimate and you don't get it... you will still be filled with joy and happiness.

The divine will be born in you according to the intensity with which you seek it. That does not mean that some supreme soul or energy from outside will enter your being. The seed is already present within you, and it will start growing. But it will grow only if you are able to give some warmth to your thirst, some heat and some fire to your thirst.

The more you long for the divine, the more is the possibility that the seed which is hidden within your heart will grow, that it will sprout and become the divine; that it will break open, that it will blossom.

If you have ever thought of experiencing the divine, if you have ever experienced a desire for silence, for truth, then know that the seed within you is longing to sprout. It means that some hidden thirst within you wants to be fulfilled. Try to understand that a very significant struggle is taking place within you; you will have to help this struggle and support it. You will have to support it because it is not enough that the seed has sprouted: a more nourishing environment is also needed. And even if the seed has sprouted, it does not mean that it will also bloom. For that, much more is needed.

Out of the many seeds scattered on the ground, only a few will grow into trees. There is this possibility in all of them: they could all sprout and grow into trees and each could in turn produce many more seeds. One small seed has the power, the potential to produce a whole forest; it contains the potential to cover the whole earth with trees. But it is also possible that the seed with this immense power and potential will be destroyed and that nothing will come out of it.

And this is only the capacity of a seed – man is capable of much more than this. One seed can create something so vast.... If a small stone can be used to create an atomic explosion...immense energy can be produced out of it. When someone experiences this fusion within his being, within his consciousness, this blossoming, this explosion, the energy and light are the experience of the divine. We don't experience the divine from the outside. The energy that we produce through this explosion of consciousness, the growth, the flowering of our being, that energy itself is the divine. And you have a thirst for this energy: this is why I welcome you.

But it does not necessarily follow that just because you have come here that you have this thirst. It is possible that you are here merely as a spectator. It is possible that you are here out of some vague curiosity – but no doors can be opened through superficial curiosity, and no secrets will be revealed to mere spectators. In life, one has to pay for everything one receives, and much has to be sacrificed.

Curiosity is of no value; this is why curiosity will not get you anywhere. Curiosity will not help you to enter into meditation. What is needed is an essential thirst for freedom, not curiosity.

Last evening I was saying to someone that if you are near an oasis and you are dying of thirst, if your thirst is intense and you reach a state where you feel that soon you will die if you don't get water, and if at that point someone offers you water but with the condition that after drinking the water you will die – that the price of the water will be your life – you will even be willing to accept this condition. When death is certain, then why not die with your thirst quenched?

If you carry this intense longing and hope within you,

then under this tremendous pressure the seed within you will break open and start growing. The seed will not sprout on its own, it needs certain conditions. It needs much pressure, much warmth for its hard outer skin to crack and the tender sprout inside to grow. Each of us has this hard covering, and if we want to come out of it, just curiosity will not do. So remember this: if you are here simply out of curiosity you will leave with that curiosity, and nothing can be done to help you. And if you are here as a spectator you will leave as one, and nothing can be done for you.

So it is necessary that each one of you look within himself to see whether or not he has an authentic longing for the divine. Each of you should ask himself this question: "Do I want to know truth?" Be very clear if your thirst for the divine is authentic, whether you have a yearning for truth, for silence, for bliss. If not, then understand that whatsoever you do here will have no meaning; it will be meaningless, without any purpose. If your meaningless efforts don't bear any fruits, meditation will not be responsible – *you* will be responsible for it.

So to begin, it is necessary that you look for an authentic seeker within you. And be clear about it: do you really seek something? And if you do, then there is a way to find it.

Buddha was once visiting a village. A man asked him, "Every day you say that everyone can become enlightened. Then why doesn't everyone become enlightened?"

"My friend," Buddha replied, "do one thing: in the evening make a list of all the people in the village and write down their desires next to their names."

The man went into the village and he asked everyone; it was a small village with only a few people, and they gave him their answers. He returned in the evening and gave the list to Buddha. Buddha asked, "How many of these people seek enlightenment?"

The man was surprised because not a single person had written that he wanted enlightenment. And Buddha said, "I say that every man is capable of enlightenment, I do not say that every man wants enlightenment."

That every man is capable of enlightenment is very different from every man wanting to be enlightened. If you want it, then consider it to be possible. If your quest is for truth, there is no power on earth that can stop you. But if you don't long for truth, then too there is no power which can give it to you.

So first you need to ask if your thirst is a real one. If so, then rest assured that a path is available. If not, then there is no path – your thirst will be your path to truth.

The second thing I would like to say by way of an introduction is that you often have a thirst for something, but you are not hopeful of ever getting what you desire. You have a desire, but you are not optimistic about it. There is the desire, but with a sense of hopelessness.

Now if the first step is taken optimistically, then the last step will also end optimistically. This too should be understood: if the first step is taken without any optimism, then the last step will end in despair. If you want the last step to be a satisfying and successful one, the first step should be taken with optimism.

I am saying that during these three days – and I will be

saying this as long as I live – you should have a very optimistic attitude. Do you realize that as far as your state of consciousness is concerned, much depends on whether your acts are rooted in positivity or negativity? If you are a pessimist to begin with, then it is as if you are sitting on the branch of a tree, and cutting the branch at the same time.

So I say to you that to be open is very important in this search. To be optimistic means you feel that if there has been a single person on this earth who has understood truth, if there has been a single person in the history of mankind who has experienced divine bliss and peace, then there is no reason why you also cannot experience it.

Don't look at the millions of people whose lives are filled with darkness, whose hopes have never seen the light of day: look at the people in history who *have* experienced truth. Don't look at the seeds which never grew into trees, which rotted and were wasted: look at those few who were successful and who experienced the divine. And remember, what was possible for those seeds is possible for every seed. What one man can experience, every other man can also experience.

Your capacity as a seed is the same as that of Buddha, of Mahavira, of Krishna or Christ. Where enlightenment is concerned nature has shown no favoritism; every man has an equal possibility. But it does not appear to be so because there are many among us who have never even tried to turn this possibility into a reality.

So to be optimistic is a basic necessity. Carry this assurance with you that if anyone has ever experienced peace, if anyone has ever experienced bliss, it is also possible for you. Don't humiliate yourself by being pessimistic. To feel pessimistic is insulting to yourself. It means that you don't see yourself as worthy of experiencing truth. And I say to you, you *are* worthy and you will certainly achieve it.

Try it and see! You have lived your whole life with a sense of hopelessness; now for these three days of the meditation camp nourish a feeling of optimism. Be as optimistic as possible that the ultimate will happen, that it will definitely happen. Why? In the outer world it is possible to approach something with optimism and not be successful. But in the inner world optimism is a very useful device. When you are full of optimism, every cell of your body is filled with optimism, every pore of your skin is filled with optimism, every breath is filled with optimism, every thought is highlighted with optimism, your lifeforce throbs with optimism and your heartbeat is suffused with optimism. When your whole being is filled with optimism, then this will create a climate in you in which the ultimate can happen.

Pessimism also creates a personality, a character where every cell is crying, is sad, is weary, is in despair, lifeless, as if one is living only in name but is dead in spirit. If this person sets out on a journey to seek something.... And the journey on the spiritual path is the greatest journey – no man has climbed a mountain peak higher than this, no man has ever dived into a deeper ocean. The depth of the self is the deepest, and the height is the highest. Someone who wants to walk this path has to be *very* optimistic.

So I say to you, for these three days maintain a very optimistic state of mind. Tonight, when you go to bed, fall asleep filled with optimism. And sleep with the assurance that tomorrow morning when you get up something will happen, something can happen, something can be done.

Have an optimistic attitude, and along with it I would also

like to say this: after many years of experience I have come to the conclusion that man's negativity can be so strong that even if he begins to achieve something, he may not be able to see it because of his negativity.

Some time ago a man used to come to me, and he would bring his wife. The first time we met he told me that his wife could not sleep. He described her condition to me: "She cannot get any sleep without medicines, and even with medicine she can only sleep for three or four hours. And my wife is afraid; strange fears seem to trouble her. She is afraid to step out of the house, and if she is in the house she is afraid that the house will collapse. If there is no one around she is afraid that if she is alone she will die, so she constantly needs someone around. At night she keeps all her medicines close to her just in case there is an emergency."

I suggested that she start doing a small meditation that would be helpful. She began to do the experiment. After seven days I met him and I asked him, "What happened? How is your wife?"

He said, "There has not been much progress – she just sleeps better."

After a week I met him again and asked him, "Any change?"

And he said, "Her condition has not changed very much, but she is a bit less afraid."

I met him again after another seven days and asked him, "Has anything happened?"

"Nothing significant," he said. "She manages to get some sleep now, is less fearful and doesn't keep the medicines close to her anymore – nothing much."

I call this a negative outlook. Even if this man were to

experience something he would not be able to see it, to recognize it. And this outlook is built into this person. It means that a negative person will not experience anything, and even if he does experience something he will not be able to recognize it – and much that might otherwise be possible will be obstructed.

In addition to having a positive approach, I also suggest that during these three days you think only about what is happening to you – don't try to think about what is not happening. In these three days whatsoever happens, watch. And forget about what does not happen, what could not happen. Just remember what you did experience. If you have even a little taste of peace, of silence, nourish that. It will give you hope and it also will push you forward. Because if you nourish something that didn't happen your momentum will be lost, and what actually did happen will also be destroyed.

So in these three days, in your experiments with meditation, pay attention to every little thing you experience and make that the basis for your progress. Don't give any energy to what doesn't happen.

Man has always been unhappy because he forgets what he has and tries to get what he cannot get. To have this kind of basis for life is absolutely wrong. Be someone who understands what he has and live on the basis of that.

I read somewhere that one man was complaining to another, "I am a very poor man, I don't have anything."

So the second man said, "If you are that poor you can do one thing: I want your right eye. I will give you five thousand rupees for it. Take these five thousand rupees and give me your right eye."

And the first man said, "That is very difficult. I cannot give my right eye."

So then the other man offered, "I will give you ten thousand rupees for both of your eyes."

Again the first man replied, "Ten thousand rupees! But still, I cannot give my eyes."

At which point the other man offered, "I will give you fifty thousand rupees if you will give me your life."

At this the first man said, "But that is impossible! I cannot give my life."

The first man said, "This shows you have many valuable things. You have two eyes which you will not sell for ten thousand rupees, and you have your life – and you were saying that you don't have anything!"

I am talking about this kind of person and this kind of thinking. Value what you have, and also what you experience through meditation, even the small things. Think about it, talk about it, because whether or not you will experience more depends on this way of thinking – and your optimism will create more. And what you don't get….

A woman used to come to me – she was well educated, a professor in a college, a Sanskrit scholar. She was attending a seven-day meditation camp, and on the first day of the camp after the meditation she came out and said to me, "Forgive me, but I did not have any communion with the divine."

It was just the first day of the experiment and she said she did not meet with the divine!

So I said, "If you had met the divine it would have been dangerous, because if you could meet the divine so easily you would not value it." And I also said, "A person would have to be really stupid to think that by sitting silently with his eyes closed for ten minutes, he will then be ready to know the divine."

So if you experience even the smallest ray of silence, consider that you have seen the whole sun because even the smallest experience of light will help you to reach to the sun. If I am sitting in a dark room and I see a thin ray of light, there are two ways I can relate to it. One way would be to say, "What is this small ray of light compared to the deep darkness surrounding me? What can one small ray of light do? – there is so much darkness all around me."

The other way would be to think, "In spite of all this darkness, there is at least one ray of light available to me, and if I go towards that ray of light I may reach the source where the sun is." This is why I am telling you not to think about all the darkness; if there is even the faintest, the tiniest ray of light, concentrate on that. It will give rise to a positive vision in you.

Usually, your life is just the opposite. If I show you a rosebush you might say, "What is there to see? Existence is so unfair, there are only three or four roses and thousands of thorns." This is one approach: to see a rosebush and say, "Existence is so unfair! There are thousands of thorns and only a few roses." This is one way of perceiving, one approach. Another way would be to say, "Existence is so mysterious: amidst those thousands of thorns it creates a rose." You could also see it like this and say, "A rose among all those thorns.... Isn't this a mysterious world! It really seems like a miracle, the possibility of a rose blooming amongst all those thorns."

So I would like to ask you to take the second approach. In these three days make your foundation from the slightest ray of hope that you see in your meditation, and let it become stronger.

The third thing is that during these three days of meditation you will not be living in the same way that you have been living up until this evening. Man is a robot, full of habits, and if one remains within the confines of one's habits, the new path to meditation will be very difficult. Hence, I suggest that you make a few changes.

One change will be that during these three days you are to talk as little as possible. Talking is the greatest affliction of this century! And you are not even aware of just how much you talk. From morning to night, until you go to sleep, you go on talking. Either you are talking to somebody else, or if there is nobody to talk to, you talk to yourself.

During these three days be conscious about stopping your habit of continuously talking. And it is just a habit. For a meditator, this is vital. During these three days I would like you to talk as little as possible, and when you do talk, it should be pure, not the ordinary chitchat that you do every day. What in fact do you talk about every day? Does it have any value? Would it be harmful to you if you didn't talk? You are simply chattering; it is not worth much. And if you didn't talk would it be harmful to others? Would others feel something is missing by not hearing what you have to say?

During these three days remember that you are not to talk much with anyone. This will be tremendously helpful. And if you do talk, it would be better if it were connected with meditation and nothing else. But it would be so much better if you did not talk at all: be in silence as much as possible.

I don't mean it to be so strict that you force yourself to be in silence, that you write what you want to say. You are free to speak, but not to chitchat. Talk consciously, and only when necessary.

This will help you in two ways. One benefit will be that you will save all the energy that is wasted by talking. Then that energy can be used for meditation. And the second benefit will be that it will disconnect you from the others and you will be in your aloneness during this time. We have come to this mountain place, and it would be a waste if all two hundred people that are gathered here were to just talk with each other, chat with each other. Then you would still be in a crowd, as you were before, and you will not be able to experience silence.

To experience silence just to be in the mountains is not enough. It is also necessary to separate yourself from others and be alone. You should make contact only if it is absolutely necessary. Imagine that you are the only person on this mountain and there is no one else around. You have to live as if you have come here alone, you are staying alone and moving around alone. Sit under a tree, alone. Don't go about in groups of people. Live separately and alone for these three days. The truth of life has never been known through living in a crowd, and it cannot be experienced like that. No experience of any significance has ever happened in a crowd. Whosoever has had a taste of silence has tasted it in absolute solitude, in aloneness.

When you stop talking to others and when all your chattering inside and outside stops, nature starts communicating with you in a mysterious way. Nature is continuously communicating with you, but you are so engrossed in your chatter that you don't hear her soft voice. You will have to quieten yourself so that you can hear the voice speaking within you.

So in these three days, talking has to be consciously reduced. If you forget and start talking out of habit and then remember again, stop right then and apologize. Be alone. You will be experimenting with this here, but you will also have to try it on your own.

Go anywhere you like, sit under a tree; you have completely forgotten that you are part of nature. You also don't know that being close to nature makes it easier to experience the ultimate; nowhere else is it easier.

So make full use of these three incredible days. Be in isolation, solitude, and don't talk unless necessary. And even if everyone is quiet, continue to be alone. A meditator has to be alone. There are very many people here, so when we all sit for meditation it may look as if there is a gathering of people meditating. But all meditation is individual, a group cannot meditate. Sitting here you are in a large group, but when you go inside yourself you will all feel alone.

When you close your eyes you will feel alone, and when you are silent there will no longer be any group. There will be two hundred people here, but each one will be only with himself and not with the other one hundred and ninety-nine meditators. Meditation cannot be done collectively. All prayer, all meditation is individual, is private.

Be alone here, and also when you leave here. And spend most of your time in silence. Don't talk. But it will not be enough to simply stop talking, you will also need to make a conscious effort to stop the constant chattering that goes on inside you. You talk to yourself, you answer yourself – quieten yourself and drop that too. If it is difficult to stop

15

this inner chatter, then firmly tell yourself to stop this noise, tell yourself that you don't like the noise.

Talk to your inner self. As a meditator, it is important to give suggestions to yourself. Try this sometime. Sit alone somewhere, tell your mind to stop its chatter, tell your mind that you don't like it, and you will be surprised to see that for a moment your inner chattering will stop.

For three days give yourself the suggestion that you will not talk. In three days you will notice the difference...that step by step, slowly, slowly the chatter is lessening.

The fourth point: you may have some complaints, some problems – you are not to pay any attention to them. If you experience a small problem or difficulty, don't give it any attention. We are not here for entertainment.

Recently, I read the story of a Chinese nun. She was visiting a village where there were only a few houses, and as it was getting dark and she was all alone she went to the area in front of all the houses and asked the villagers, "Please let me stay in one of your houses."

She was a stranger to them, and besides that she was of a different religion, so the villagers closed their doors to her.

The next village was very far away, and it was dark and she was alone. So she had to spend the night in a field and she slept under a cherry tree. In the middle of the night she woke up – it was cold, and because of this she could not sleep. She looked up and saw that the flowers had all blossomed; the tree was covered with flowers. And the moon had risen, and the moonlight was very beautiful. She experienced a moment of immense joy.

16

In the morning she went back to the village and thanked all the people who had refused to give her shelter for the night. When they asked her, "For what?" she said, "For your love, for your compassion and kindness in closing your doors to me last night. Because of this I was able to experience a moment of unbelievable joy. I saw the cherry flowers in bloom and the moon in its glory, and I saw something that I had never seen before. If you had given me shelter I would not have seen it. That's when I realized your kindness, your reason for closing all your doors to me."

This is one way to look at things. It is possible that you also might have been sent away from each door that night, and that you might have felt angry all night. You might have felt so much hatred, so much anger towards those people that perhaps you might not have noticed the flowers blossoming in the cherry tree and you would not have seen the moon rising, let alone experienced a feeling of gratitude. You would not have experienced any of these things.

There is another way to relate to life – and that is when you are filled with gratitude for everything in life. And you must remember that during these three days, feel gratitude for everything. Feel gratitude for what you receive and don't be bothered about what you don't receive. This is the basis of gratitude. It is on this base that carefreeness and simplicity are born inside you.

To summarize, I would like to say that in these three days you will relentlessly try to go inside, to meditate and to enter into silence. On this journey, a very firm resolve is needed. The conscious mind where all the thought processes take place is only a small part; the rest of the mind is still deeper. If we were to divide the mind into ten parts, the conscious mind would be only one part, the other nine parts are the unconscious mind. Our thinking and reasoning take place in only one part, but the rest of the brain is not aware of this. The rest of the brain has no sense of it. When we make a conscious resolution to meditate, to enter into *samadhi,* ultimate bliss, the major part of our brain remains ignorant of this resolution. This unconscious part will not support us in this resolution. But if we don't get support from it we cannot succeed. To get the support, a determined, conscious effort is needed. I will now explain how to make this conscious effort.

When you wake up, let it be with determination, and at night when you go to bed, when you lie down on your bed, think over your resolution for five minutes and repeat it to yourself as you go to sleep.

I would like to explain this exercise for becoming determined, and you will be practicing it here as well as in your normal life. As I explained, with this resolution your whole mind, conscious and unconscious both, is to decide that, "I will be silent, I am determined to experience meditation."

The night Gautam Buddha attained enlightenment, he was sitting under his *bodhi* tree and he said, "I will not get up from this place until I am enlightened."

You might think, "But what is the connection? How will not getting up help him to get enlightened?" But the resolution, "I will not…" spreads all through the body – and he did not get up until he became enlightened! Amazingly, he became enlightened the same night. And he had been trying for six years, but never before did he have such intensity.

I will give you a small exercise to intensify your resolve.

We will do this exercise here and also at night before sleeping.

If you exhale completely and then stop yourself from inhaling, what will happen? If I exhale completely and then pinch my nose shut and don't inhale, what will happen? In a little while my total being will struggle to inhale. Won't every pore of my body and those millions of cells scream for air? The longer I try to hold my breath, the deeper the longing for breath is going to spread into my unconscious mind. The longer I hold my breath, the more the innermost part of my being is going to ask for air. And if I hold it to the last moment, my whole being will demand air. Now it is not a simple desire anymore; the top layer is not the only one affected. Now it has become a question of life and death; now the deeper layers, the layers underneath, are also going to demand more air.

In that moment, when you reach the state where your whole being is starving for air, you should repeat to yourself, "I am going to experience meditation." In that moment, when your life is demanding air, you should repeat the thought, "I will enter into a state of silence. This is my resolution: I will experience meditation." In this state, your mind should repeat this thought; your body will ask for air and your mind will repeat this thought. The stronger the demand for air, the deeper your resolution will enter inside. And if your whole being is struggling and you are repeating this sentence, then the strength of your resolution will increase many times over. In this way it will reach to your unconscious mind.

You will be making this resolution every day before the daily meditation, and at night you will do it before going to sleep. Repeat the sentence, and then go to sleep. When you are falling asleep, at that moment also let it be constantly ringing in your mind: "I will experience meditation. This is my resolution. I will enter into silence."

This resolution should go on ringing in your mind so that you don't even realize when you are falling asleep. In sleep your conscious mind is inactive and the doors are open for the unconscious mind. If your mind repeats this idea again and again while the conscious mind is inactive, it can then enter the subconscious mind. And in time you will observe a significant change – you will see it even in these three days. So now try to understand the method by which you can strengthen the resolution.

✳ This is the way to do it: first take slow, deep breaths, filling yourself up, filling your lungs up as deeply as you can. When you have inhaled as much as you can, continue to hold the thought, "I will experience meditation," and keep repeating this sentence. Then exhale, and at one point you will feel that there is no more air to exhale. But there is – so throw that out too and repeat the sentence. Now you will feel that there is absolutely no more air left – but still there is, so throw that out. Don't be afraid: you will never exhale completely. That's why, when you feel that there is no more breath left in you, there always is – so try also to exhale that. Exhale as totally as you can, and keep repeating, "I will experience meditation."

It is a strange phenomenon: through it a thought process is triggered in your unconscious mind. An intense resolve will arise and you will already see its effects tomorrow, so you have to make your resolution very strong. We will start the experiment before we leave this place this evening. You are to do it five times, that is, you should inhale and exhale five times and repeat the thought inside five times. If anyone has a heart problem, or any other problem, don't do it strenuously, do it softly. Do it as gently as possible, don't make yourself uncomfortable.

I have talked about the will to experience. You must practice it every night during these three days, before sleeping. Lying on your bed, repeat the sentence as you gradually fall asleep. If you follow this process diligently and your voice reaches the unconscious, the result is easy to induce and is unmistakable.

I wanted to talk about these few things today, and I hope you have already understood the points that are relatively important. As I have said, there should be no talking. Naturally, you will not read the newspaper or listen to the radio, because that would also be a kind of talking.

Or when I said you will be silent and alone...this means that you avoid the company of people as much as you can. Except for the time when we gather here, or when we eat... but then too you will be quiet and in silence. There should be total silence, as if you are not there at all. When you come here to meditate, then too you will come in silence. You will see the results of three days in silence. When you walk on the street be quiet; when sitting, standing, moving around, be quiet. And most of the time try to be alone. Select a beautiful place and sit there quietly. And if there is someone with you, they too should sit quietly; don't talk, otherwise the mountains are wasted, the beauty is wasted. You will not see that which is right in front of you. You will destroy everything with your talking. Be alone.

I wanted to mention these few things which are important for everyone. If there is no thirst within you, and there seems to be no way to awaken this thirst, then tell me about this tomorrow. Let me know if you are not very hopeful about yourself and you don't feel there can be any hope, or if you find it difficult to strengthen your resolve and feel it is not possible for you to meditate. So tomorrow you can ask me about the difficulties that you think you will face in the next three days, so that no time is wasted later on.

If you have any personal problem, any pain or sorrow which you want to be relieved of which is preventing you from meditating, or if you are coming across any difficulty while meditating, remember this: you can ask your question separately. It will not be for everyone; it will be for you individually, that you follow a separate procedure. And whatever problem you may have, be clear about it tomorrow morning so that we will be prepared for the next three days. I wanted to say these few things.

You have to maintain a single-pointed vision. And then from tomorrow we will start with what is to be done, we will begin the real work tomorrow.

Now we will sit a little apart from each other – the hall is big enough so that everyone can spread out – and we will make our resolutions before we leave here.

...Not so jerkily, very slowly, slowly filling the lungs completely. When you fill your lungs, repeat to yourself, "I will experience meditation." Repeat this sentence. Then, when the lungs are filled to the maximum, hold your breath for a while, repeating the sentence. You may get nervous, you will feel like exhaling, but continue to hold your breath and repeat the sentence. Then slowly start exhaling, again repeating the sentence. Keep exhaling until you feel you are empty, and then go on exhaling and repeating the sentence. When you feel absolutely empty, hold this emptiness. Don't inhale yet, and go on repeating the sentence as long as you can. And then, slowly begin to inhale. An inhalation plus an exhalation is one round. Everyone should follow this procedure slowly, step by step.

After doing it five times straighten your back, breathe slowly, sit quietly and relax for five minutes. We will do this exercise for ten minutes and then everyone will leave this place silently. Remember, you are not to talk, and this is from now on. In that sense the meditation camp begins right now. When you go to bed repeat this exercise from five to seven times, as long as you feel comfortable, then switch off the light.and fall asleep. Fall asleep thinking, "I will be in silence, this is my aim." And when sleep envelops you this thought will be with you.

When you have finished doing the exercise five times, rest quietly for a while and breathe softly. Now keep your back straight. Let your body be loose. Your back is straight and your body relaxed. Close your eyes. Quietly take a deep breath and do as I have just said five times: "I will experience silence. I will experience meditation. I am determined that I will experience meditation." Let your whole being make this oath that you will enter into meditation. Let your whole being resonate with it. This should reach to the deepest layer of your consciousness.

After doing this five times, very softly, very relaxedly, sit up, straighten your back and slow down your breathing. Exhale slowly and keep on watching your breathing. Rest for five minutes. During this rest period the resolution that you have made will sink deeper inside you. Make the resolution five times, then, sitting quietly, watch your breath for five minutes and take slow breaths.

THE PATH OF MEDITATION

begin with the body

Chapter 2

My Beloved Ones,

*L*AST NIGHT I spoke about how to create a foundation for meditation within yourself. My approach to meditation is not based on any scriptures, any holy books or any specific school of thought. I am only talking about the paths which I have walked on and which I have known by going within myself. This is why what I am saying is not just a theory. And when I invite you to try it, I have no doubt that you will also be successful in finding what you are longing for. Rest assured that I will only talk about that which I have experienced.

I have had to go through a period of intense anguish and suffering. I had to go through a period of trial and error, and during that period I struggled to go inside myself. I made a constant effort to try all the roads, all the paths in this direction.

Those days were very painful, full of anguish and suffering. But there was constant effort, and because of this effort – just as when a great waterfall is falling from a great height and the constant flow wears away even the rocks – so just like a waterfall, with continuous effort, somewhere I found an opening. And I will only talk about the methods through which I found this opening.

So I can say to you with absolute confidence and assurance that if you try this method the result is absolutely guaranteed. At the time, there was pain and sorrow, but now there is no pain or sorrow within me.

Yesterday somebody asked me, "People ask you about so many of their problems. Aren't you troubled by them?"

I said to him, "If the problem is not yours, then you cannot be troubled by it. If the problem belongs to someone else then there is no trouble in it. The trouble starts if you take the problem as your own."

In this sense I don't have any problems. But I experience a different type of sadness, and that is that I see many people around me who appear to be in so much pain, who have so many problems, and I feel that their pain and trouble can so easily be removed because there are such simple solutions to them. I feel that if they were to knock on the door, the door would open so easily. And yet they are standing right in front of it, crying. That's when I experience a very different kind of anguish and suffering.

There is a short Parsi story:

A blind man and his friend were crossing a desert. They were going on different journeys but they must have met on the way, and the other man must have asked the blind man to join him. They were together for some days and their friendship deepened over that time. One morning the blind man got up earlier than his friend and felt around for his stick. It was a desert night and it was very cold, it was winter time. He did not find the stick, but there was a snake which had stiffened because of the cold so the blind man picked it up and thanked God saying, "I had lost my stick but now you have given me a better, a smoother stick." He thanked

God and said, "You are very compassionate."

Then he poked his friend with this stick to wake him, saying, "Get up, it's morning."

When the friend got up and saw the snake, he became afraid and said, "What is that you are holding in your hand? Drop it immediately! It is a snake, it is dangerous!"

The blind man replied, "Friend, in a fit of jealousy you are calling my beautiful stick a snake. You want me to throw it away so that you can take it – I may be blind, but I'm not stupid."

His friend replied, "Are you mad? Have you gone mad? Throw it away immediately! It is a snake and it is dangerous!"

But the blind man said, "You have stayed with me for so many days and you still haven't understood how smart I am. I had lost my stick and now the Almighty has given me a more beautiful stick, and you are just trying to fool me by calling it a snake."

The blind man, in his anger, thought that his friend was jealous and envious, and so he started off on his own. After a little while the sun came up and the snake warmed up and came back to life. It was no longer cold and it bit the blind man.

The pain I'm talking about is the same pain that the blind man's friend must have felt for his friend. Just like him, I also feel pain for the people all around. They are carrying a snake in their hands, not a stick, but if I tell them they wonder what jealousy is provoking me to say this. And I am not talking about someone else, I am talking about *you*.

Don't think I'm talking about the person sitting next to

you, I am talking absolutely to you. And I can see snakes in all your hands; yet anything that only looks like a stick is of no help, it is not a stick. But I don't want you to leave the path. And I don't want you to think that in a jealous state I am trying to snatch away your beautiful stick, so I don't directly call it a snake. Slowly, slowly I am trying to make you understand that what you are holding on to is wrong.

And in fact I am not even saying that what you are holding on to is wrong. All I am saying is that there is something higher to hold on to. There is greater joy to be experienced, there are greater truths in life to be understood. What you are now holding on to can only lead to your destruction.

What we spend our lives doing eventually destroys us, destroys our entire lives. And when our whole lives have been destroyed, when our whole life is finished, there is only one pain and one sorrow that man suffers at the moment of death – and that is his regret at losing a very precious life.

So today, the first thing I would like to say is that the thirst of which I spoke last night will arise only when you see, when you realize that the life you are leading right now is wrong. That thirst will arise only when you realize that the way you are living your life right now is absolutely wrong, meaningless. Is this such a difficult thing to understand? And do you know with any certainty that what you have collected so far has any value? Do you know for sure whether you will be able to know immortality with what you have accumulated? With all the efforts you are making in all directions, do you really know that you are not just building sandcastles, or is there some solid foundation to it? Think this over, contemplate on it.

When you start to reflect and question life, a thirst begins to arise in you. A thirst for truth arises out of contemplation. There are very few who think about life, *very* few. Most people live life like driftwood floating down a river: it just keeps on floating and goes wherever the river takes it. If the river takes it towards the bank, it floats towards the bank; if it takes it midstream, it floats towards the middle of the river as if it had no life, a destination of its own. Most of us live the life of a piece of wood floating in the river – we go wherever time and circumstances take us.

Thinking about life and its purpose will help you to find a direction: whether you should live the life of a piece of wood floating in the river, whether you should live like a dried leaf which blows wherever the wind takes it, or whether you should be an individual, a person, a thinking person, one who has a direction in life, one who has decided what he wants to become and what he should be, one who has taken his life and its unfoldment into his own hands.

Man's greatest creation is himself; his greatest creation will be his own self-realization. Anything else that he creates will not be of much value. It will be like drawing a line on water. But that which he creates inside himself, that which he makes of himself, will be like a carving in stone: it can never be erased, it will be with him forever.

So think about your life – are you a piece of wood floating in the river? Are you a dead leaf which is picked up and blown around by the wind? If you think about this, you will see that you are just floating like a piece of wood, and you will see that you are being blown around like one of the dead leaves on the ground, carried by the wind to wherever it is blowing. Right now the streets are covered with these leaves. Have you made any conscious progress in your life, or have you just been pushed around by the wind? And if you have been pushed around by the wind, have you reached anywhere? Has anyone ever reached anywhere like this? If there is no consciously chosen goal in life, one reaches nowhere. The thirst for a conscious goal will arise in you only if you think about it, reflect on it, meditate on it.

You must have heard this story about Buddha. This story is about how Buddha renounced his life, about how he became an ascetic and how the desire for truth arose in him. It is a very famous story, and very meaningful.

When Buddha was a child his parents were told that their son would one day become either a great king, an emperor, or a great monk. So his father arranged everything so that Buddha would never experience any sorrow and should never feel like renouncing his life. He built a palace for him using all the artistry and craftsmanship of those times and with all kinds of luxuries, gardens....

And there were different palaces, one for every season, and he gave orders to all the servants that Buddha should never see even a wilted flower; so that he would not come to know that flowers can die and the question, "Maybe I too will die?" would never arise in him. So during the night all the dead flowers would be removed from the garden. Any weak tree would be uprooted and removed. Only young people were allowed to be around him; old people were not allowed to enter because Buddha might think, "Man becomes old...one day maybe I too will become old."

Until he grew up to be a young man, he did not know anything about death. He had never heard about death.

He was kept totally ignorant of the people that were dying in his village so that he would not think, "If people die, then maybe I too will die one day."

I'm trying to explain the meaning of contemplation. Contemplation means to reflect on whatever is happening around you. If death is happening right in front of you, then contemplate on whether it will happen to you too. If you see someone who is old, then contemplate on whether this will also happen to you.

Buddha's father tried in every way to prevent this kind of contemplation from happening in him – I want you to do everything so that this contemplation will arise in you. The father did everything he could to prevent Buddha from thinking, but still it happened.

One day Buddha went out and saw an old man walking on the street. He asked his attendant, "What has happened to this man? Do other people look like this too?"

The attendant said, "I cannot lie to you – everyone has to become old like him one day."

Buddha immediately asked, "Me too?"

The attendant said, "My lord, I cannot lie to you, no one is excluded."

Buddha said, "Take me back to the palace! I now understand that I too can become old. If this is going to happen tomorrow, then there is nothing left."

This is what I call contemplation. But the attendant said, "We are going to a youth festival, the whole village will be waiting for us. Let's go on."

Buddha said, "I have no wish to go. The youth festival has no meaning because everybody will get old one day."

They went a little further on and saw a funeral procession.

Buddha asked, "What is this? What are these people doing? What are they carrying on their shoulders?"

The attendant was hesitant to answer. He said, "I should not tell you, but I cannot lie to you. This man has died, he has died and these people are taking him away."

Buddha asked, "What is it to die?" For the first time he came to know that people die.

Buddha said, "Now I have no wish to go, take me back immediately! It is not this man who has died – rather, I have died."

This is what I call contemplation. A man has succeeded in contemplation if he understands that what has happened to someone else can also happen to him one day. People who don't understand what is happening all around them are blind, and in a way we are all blind. This is why I have told you the story of the blind man who was carrying a snake in his hand.

So the first thing for you to do – and it is very important – is to observe all that is happening around you, and through this an understanding will arise in you. Therefore the first, the most important thing for you to do, will be to observe everything around you. Through this observation a quest will arise in you, a question will arise, and this will in turn give rise to a thirst for a higher truth. I have suffered much pain. When that pain subsided, in its place I began to see the steps on the path. Now I want to talk about the first step on this path.

I have come to understand that two things are necessary if you want to attain to the ultimate consciousness, to the divine, to your inner being. One is the circumference, the circumference of meditation. The other important thing is the center of meditation – the circumference of meditation and the center of meditation; or you can call it the body of meditation and the soul of meditation. Today I will talk about the circumference of meditation, tomorrow I will talk about the soul or the center, and the day after tomorrow about the fruits of meditation. Just these three things: the circumference of meditation, the center and the fruits of meditation. In other words, the foundation of meditation, meditation itself and the fulfillment of it.

The foundation of meditation involves only your periphery, and the periphery of your personality is the body. Hence the periphery of meditation involves only the body. So the first step towards meditation begins with your body. So remember, whatever negative feelings you may have about your body which other people may have imprinted on you, drop them. The body is just an instrument in the material as well as in the spiritual world.

The body is neither an enemy nor a friend, it is just an instrument you can use to do wrong or you can use to do good. Through it you can either get involved in the material life or you can get involved in the ultimate. The body is just an instrument. Don't hold any misconceptions about it. People usually believe that the body is antagonistic towards us, that it is sinful, that it is our enemy and that it needs to be suppressed. I tell you that this is wrong – the body is neither an enemy nor a friend; it is what you make it. That is why the body is so mysterious, so extraordinary.

In the world, whenever something wrong has happened it has happened through the body, and whenever something right has happened it has happened through the body. The body is only the means, the instrument.

So for meditation it is necessary to start with attention to the body, because you cannot proceed without first putting this instrument in order. If the body is not in the right condition you cannot proceed. So the first step is to purify the body; the purer the body, the easier it will be to go deeper inside.

What does purifying the body mean? The first meaning is that there should be no disturbance, no blocks, no complexes in the body, in the system of the body – then the body is pure.

Try to understand how these complexes and blockages enter the body. If the body is without any blocks, if it doesn't have any disturbances and if there are no problems, no interferences, then the body is pure and helps you to go inside. But if you are very angry, if you get angry and you are not expressing it, the heat that this creates will accumulate in some part of your body and it will become a blockage. You must have seen how anger can lead to hysteria, how it can lead to illness. Recent experiments being done on the human body show that out of a hundred diseases, fifty of these are not of the body but of the mind. But the mental illnesses become disturbances in the body, and if there is a disturbance in the body, if the body is not healthy, then the body's whole system becomes rigid and impure.

All the different schools of spiritual discipline and the different religions have tried many incredible and revolutionary experiments to purify the body, and it will be good to understand these experiments. If you try these experiments, in a few days you will discover just how mysterious your body is. Your body will not appear to be an enemy, it will be a temple where the divine resides. Then it will not be an enemy but a friend, and you will feel grateful to it. The body is not you. It is made of matter. You and your body are different from each other. Yet you can make tremendous use of it, and then you will feel gratitude towards it, you will feel indebted to it because it is so supportive.

Keeping the body free of blockages is the first step towards purifying the body. And there are many blockages in our bodies. For instance, a few days ago a man came and said to me, "For some days now I have been doing some meditations of a particular religion, and the mind has become very quiet."

I said to him, "I don't think your mind is quiet."

He said, "How can you say that?"

I replied, "Since you arrived you have been jiggling both your legs about." He was sitting and jiggling his legs. I said, "It is not possible for the mind to be silent when the legs are jiggling about so much."

The agitation of the body comes from the agitation of the mind. When the movement of the mind slows down, the body too slows down. The bodies of Buddha and Mahavira would have appeared to be like the stone that their statues are made of; they would have appeared stone-like. It is not coincidental that their statues are made of stone. The reason for it is that they had started looking like stone, all movement inside them had stopped. That is, they moved only when necessary; otherwise they remained absolutely still.

When your legs jiggle, it is the energy created by your dissatisfaction which is not finding any outlet and you dissipate it by jiggling your legs. When a man is angry he gnashes his teeth and he clenches his fists – why? His eyes turn red – why? Why the fists? Even when you are alone and angry at someone you will clench your fist. There is no one to hit, but the energy that is created by your anger has to be released somehow. The muscles in your hands become tense and so the energy is released.

These difficulties have been created by social conditioning. A man without conditioning has a purer body than yours. A wild man's body is purer than your bodies; it does not have any blockages because where you suppress your emotions, he expresses his emotions very easily and spontaneously.

Imagine you are at work and your boss says something to you and you become angry, but you cannot tighten your fists. Now what will happen to all this energy which has just been created in you? And remember this: the energy does not simply evaporate. Energy is never destroyed, energy never comes to an end. If you say something to me which makes me angry, I will not be able to express my anger in front of all these people. I cannot gnash my teeth or clench my fist; I cannot call you names or jump around in anger or pick up a stone. What happens to the energy that has been generated inside me? – this energy will cripple a part of my body. It will be used to create a blockage in some part of my body; a disharmony will form. By that I mean that most of our disharmonies emerge in the body.

You may be surprised, and you might say that you don't see any such blockages. But I ask you to try an experiment; you will then discover how many blockages there are in your body. Have you ever noticed that if you are in a room alone you may clench your teeth, or when you look in the mirror you may stick out your tongue or widen your eyes in anger?

You may even laugh at yourself for doing this. Sometimes it may happen that while you are taking a shower you will suddenly jump, and you will wonder, "Why did I jump? Why did I clench my teeth at my reflection in the mirror? Why do I feel like humming a song?"

My suggestion to you is that once a week, for half an hour, you lock yourself in a room and let your body do whatsoever it feels like doing. You will be surprised! Your body may start dancing – let it do whatsoever it pleases, don't stop it. It may dance, it may jump or even scream. Or it may jump at an imaginary enemy, it is possible. Then you will wonder, "What is happening?" All these are the disharmonies of the body that are repressed but are still very much present and want to be expressed, but your social conditioning does not allow it. You also don't allow them to be expressed, so in this way many disharmonies have found a home in your body. And if the body is full of blockages it is not healthy and you cannot go inside.

So the first step in meditation will be to purify the body, and the first step in purifying the body will be to put an end to all the disorders in the body. So you will have to stop accumulating new disorders and also find a way to release the old ones. A solution is that once or twice a month you lock yourself in a room and let your body do whatever it feels like doing. If you feel like removing all your clothes and dancing naked, then do it, then throw off your clothes. You will be surprised that after half an hour of all that jumping you will feel so relaxed, so quiet and fresh. It will seem strange but you will feel very silent, and you will wonder where this silence has come from. When you exercise or take a walk you feel a lightness – why is that? It is

38

because many of the blocks in the body are released.

Do you know why sometimes you are just looking for someone to get into a fight with? Why you are so ready to fight that you jump on the first person who comes along? It is because you have collected so many energy blocks and they are all wanting to be released. Whenever there is a war – there have been two world wars – during these world wars people were really hooked on reading their daily newspaper first thing in the morning. And many curious things happen in wartime. You may not know that during these wars two very strange things happened: one was that there was a drop in the number of suicides all over the world.

During the First and Second World Wars, psychologists were surprised at this phenomenon. During the whole time of the wars there were very few suicides; all over the world there was a drop in the number of suicides, and psychologists were puzzled. During that period there were also fewer murders. And another strange thing, there was also a decline in mental illness during the time of the war. Later they realized that all the news about the war and the intensity of the news had helped to release certain blocks in people.

Somehow, when you hear any news about war you get involved with it. For instance, your anger.... Now imagine you are angry with Hitler, so you build an effigy of Hitler and burn it, shout slogans and scream at him. You can sit in your living room and abuse him. Hitler is not there in front of you, he is an illusionary enemy. But in this way many of your blockages are released and it will result in better psychological health. You will be surprised: consciously you don't want there to be war, but deep inside you do want it to happen. During wartime people seem to be very cheerful.

Although danger may be very close by, still people seem to be cheerful.

Some time ago India was attacked by China: there was a sudden burst of energy in all of you at the time. Do you know why? The reason was that a lot of the blocks in your bodies were released through your anger and that made you feel very light. Wars will always be fought; there will be wars as long as there are people with unhealthy bodies. Wars will not end until everyone's body becomes so pure that there are no blockages in them that need wars to dissolve them. What I am telling you right now will sound very strange, but there will be war in the world as long as people's bodies are unhealthy. No matter how much effort is made to stop war, you will still derive a certain pleasure from it.

And you also experience pleasure from fighting. Think about it: don't you get some kind of pleasure out of fighting? The fight can be at any level – it can be between one religion and another, between a Hindu and a Mohammedan – and you will be surprised that it has no basis. Just look, whenever a religion is born it is divided into twenty other sub-sects, and then each of these is divided into sub-branches. Why? – because man's body is so unhealthy, it is so filled with disharmony that he is just looking for any excuse. People grab at even the smallest excuse to fight, because fighting gives them some release and makes them feel more relaxed.

The first step of moving towards meditation is the purification of the body.

I would also like to add two more things. In order to release all the old disorders, one method is to let yourself go totally wild in a closed room, dropping all the ideas that you have forced on yourself. Drop them! Then let it all happen and observe your body and see what it does. It dances, it jumps, it falls to the floor and lies there. It hits an imaginary enemy. It pretends to stab someone, to shoot someone. Observe everything it does and let it happen. A month or two of this experiment and you will be surprised at the results. You will find that your body has become very easy, healthy and pure. It has found a release; the old blocks will have found an outlet.

In days gone by, seekers used to go into the forests. They liked to be in solitude and did not want to be in a crowd. One of the main reasons for this was for purification. You have no idea what Buddha or Mohammed did when they went into solitude; there is not one book that tells you what they did when they were in the forests. So what do you suppose they were doing? I tell you without a doubt that they must have been purifying their bodies. The word 'mahavira' means someone whose blocks have been destroyed – and the first step towards destroying these blocks is in the body.

So first those blocks that you have accumulated have to be released. In the beginning you will find it strange, and if you feel like laughing at yourself for behaving like a madman, jumping around, then allow the laughter to happen. If you feel like crying then let it happen. If I tell you right now to let go, then some of you will start laughing. There is pain within you which could not be expressed, which was suppressed, and it will come out. Or there is laughter waiting to come out that was stopped; it is lodged in your body in the form of a blockage. Now it will come out. You will feel that what is happening is absurd, but let it happen. Try this method of body purification on your own, and the upper layer of your blockages will be removed and you will feel lighter.

41

The second thing: you have to see to it that new blocks don't develop. I have spoken about how to release the old blocks, but you go on accumulating new blocks every day. I may say something that makes you very angry, but you will not show it because of your social conditioning and social etiquette. A fireball of energy will move into your body. Where will it go? It may create stress on some nerves, disrupt them, lodge itself there. This is why there is a difference between the eyes and face of someone who is angry and of someone who is peaceful: the fever of anger has not distorted anything in a peaceful man's face. The body blooms into its true beauty only when there is no disharmony in it. In that sense, a beautiful body is simply an indication that there is no disharmony. That's when the eyes become beautiful, and even the ugliest body seems to be beautiful.

Gandhi's body was very ugly when he was young, but as he grew older he started looking more beautiful. It was very strange. The beauty was not of the body, it was the result of the dissolving of all the blocks in the body. Very few people understood when they saw this. There's no doubt that Gandhi was ugly; if we measure by any criterion of beauty, he could not have been considered beautiful. If you see photographs of him as a child and as a young man you will see that he was ugly, but as he grew older he started looking more and more beautiful. If you have led your life beautifully, then your youth is not as beautiful as your old age. Because in youth there are many forces working in you, in old age all the feverishness disappears. If you have lived, your life beautifully then old age is the most beautiful part of life, because then all the feverishness is gone. All the disorders will have disappeared if you have developed rightly and lived your life totally.

Have you ever wondered how all these blockages accumulate in your body? If I insult you and you get angry, this creates a surge of energy in you. And energy cannot be destroyed, energy is never destroyed. Energy has to be used, and if it is not used it will become perverted and self-destructive. You have to use it – but how to use this energy?

Imagine you are at work and you are angry – there is a strong feeling of anger in you and you cannot express it. I suggest you try this: transform that energy creatively. Contract the muscles of your legs – nobody can see your legs – as much as you can. Make them stiff, pull them as tight as you can. When you feel that you can't go any further, suddenly relax them. You will be surprised to see that the anger has gone, and you will also be exercising your muscles and toning them up. And that angry impulse which could have become destructive has been released, and in the bargain your legs have been toned up. You can tone up and improve whichever part of your body has become blocked by anger, and the energy which has been created will be used in a creative way. If your hands are blocked, tighten the muscles of both your hands and all the energy of anger will be used. If your stomach is blocked, pull all the muscles of your stomach in and imagine that all the energy of your anger is being used to contract these muscles. You will see that in a minute or two the anger will have disappeared and the energy will have been used creatively.

Energy is always neutral. The energy which is created by anger is not destructive in itself; it is destructive only because it is being used in the form of anger. Make better use of it. And if it is not used in a better way it will continue to exist in a destructive form. It cannot disappear unless you do something. If you can learn to make use of it, it can bring a revolution into your life.

So to purify the body old blocks have to be released and new blocks have to be transformed creatively. These are the two preliminary steps and they are very important. Most of the postures in yoga, the *asanas*, are meant for using the body creatively. Physical exercise makes creative use of the body. If you don't use your body creatively, then all this energy which could have been a blessing will become a curse. You are all suffering from your own energy; in other words, just having energy has become a problem, a burden.

There was an incident in Jesus' life. He was leaving a village when he saw a man on a rooftop screaming and shouting obscenities. Jesus climbed a ladder and asked him, "My friend, what are you doing? Why are you wasting your life in this ugly way? You seem to be drunk."

The man opened his eyes and recognized Jesus. He got up and bowed to Jesus and said, "My lord, I was very ill, I was near death. You blessed me and made me well. Have you forgotten? Now I am perfectly well, but what do I do with all this good health? This is why I drink."

Jesus was surprised. The man said, "Now I am healthy, what am I supposed to do with this good health? So I drink and somehow I manage." Hearing this, Jesus felt great sadness and he climbed down from the ladder.

Then he went into the village where he saw a man chasing after a prostitute. He stopped the man and asked him, "Friend, why are you misusing your eyes in this way?"

The man recognized Jesus and said, "Have you forgotten me? I was blind and you touched me, then I was able to see again. Now what am I to do with my eyes?"

Jesus was very sad as he left the village. Outside the village a man was beating his chest and crying. Jesus touched him on the head and asked, "Why are you crying? There is so much beauty in the world. Life is not for crying."

The man recognized Jesus and said, "You have forgotten! I died and people were about to bury me, and then with your miracle you brought me back to life. Now what should I do with my life?"

This story seems to be completely fictitious, untrue – but what *are* you doing? What are you doing with your life? Whatever energy you have collected in your life, you are only using it to destroy yourself. Life has only two paths: if the energy that we have available to us in our mind and body is used destructively, then this is the path to hell; if the same energy can be used creatively, this is the path to heaven. Creativity is heaven and destructiveness is hell. If you make creative use of your energy you will start moving closer to heaven, and if you use your energies destructively you will be going towards hell – there is no other meaning of heaven and hell.

Consider what you are doing. Do you know how much energy is triggered within someone when he gets angry? Do you know that in a rage even a weak man can lift a rock that he would not even dream of lifting when he is calm? An angry man can overpower a strong but calm man in a moment.

Once it happened in Japan.... There was a group of people called *samurai*, the warriors of that country who made their living by the sword. Life and death was a game to them. One of the samurai was a great warrior and he was chief of the army. Then his wife fell in love with one of the servants in their house. It was a custom that if your wife fell in love with some other man he would be challenged to a duel. That meant that one of them would be killed, and whoever won the duel would also get the wife.

So the servant was in love with the wife of this great samurai warrior, and the warrior said to him, "You fool, now there is no other way but to fight a duel to the death. Now we have to fight. Tomorrow morning, come with a sword."

The servant was very scared. His master was a very strong man and he was just a servant, sweeping and dusting; how could he fight with a sword? He had never even touched a sword. He said, "How can I lift a sword?"

The samurai replied, "Now there is no way out. Tomorrow you will have to fight with a sword."

He went home and he was thinking about it all night long. There was no escape. He picked up a sword next morning – he had never touched a sword – and left the house. People were shocked to see him, because when he arrived at the place for the duel he looked like a flaming fire. The samurai became nervous when he saw him, and he asked the servant, "Do you even know how to lift a sword?" – he didn't even hold the sword in the right way.

The servant said, "There is no question now, my death is certain. And since it is certain that I am going to be killed, then I will try to win. Death is certain, so I will try to kill you."

And it was an unusual duel: the warrior was killed and the servant won! When the servant realized that his death was certain and that there was no escape, it created a tremendous burst of energy in him. He did not know how to fight with a sword and so he did just the opposite of what was expected, and it put him in even more danger. But when he saw the force of his attack, his anger, his presence, the warrior retreated. All his expertise was useless because he was fighting very calmly. For him this was nothing, for him fighting was a very ordinary thing. He kept moving back until he was killed by the sheer force of the servant's energy. He died, and the man who was absolutely ignorant, who was totally unfamiliar with this art, won.

Anger or any other emotion gives you much energy. Every living cell in your body generates energy, and there are many areas of stored energy in the body. These are for emergencies, as safety measures, and they are not used every day.

If I ask you to participate in a race, no matter how hard you try you will not run as fast as you would if someone were chasing you with a gun. The point is that at such times, the energy which is stored for an emergency is released into the bloodstream. At such times the body is bathed with energy. If this energy is not used creatively, then it will harm you, it will destroy you.

In this world it is not the weak people who commit crimes, it is the strong ones; they are forced to because they have so much energy. The truth is that weak people cannot do much harm, but people who are strong can do much harm because they don't know how to use their energy creatively. So all criminals can be considered to be a source of much energy. If they were given support their energy could be transformed in an amazing way. You must be aware that in history there have been many incidents where a sinner has suddenly been transformed into a saint. There was simply so much energy that needed transformation and then everything would change.

Angulimal had committed many murders. He made a vow to kill one thousand people. He had already killed nine hundred and ninety-nine people, and he wore a necklace made out of their fingers. He needed only one more man. Whenever people heard that Angulimal was around they would leave, because nobody wanted to be near him. He would not look at the person, he would not think even for a moment – he would simply kill whomsoever he could find. Even King Prasanjit of Bihar was afraid of him; he would shiver just at the mention of his name. He sent many soldiers after him but Angulimal could not be captured.

One day Buddha was passing through that hilly region. The people of the village told him, "Don't go there! You are a peaceful monk and Angulimal will kill you."

Buddha said, "I have chosen my path to walk, and I won't change it for any reason. If Angulimal is there then there is an even greater need for me to go there. It remains to be seen whether Angulimal will kill me or I will kill him."

But the people said, "This is absolute madness! You don't even have a weapon, how are you going to kill Angulimal?"

Buddha was not a man of violence, and Angulimal was huge, an almost demon-like man. But Buddha said, "Now we have to see whether Angulimal kills Buddha, or Buddha kills Angulimal. And I will walk only on my chosen path. Once I select a path I don't change it. And it is all the more fortunate because I will have an opportunity to meet Angulimal. It is an unexpected opportunity."

So Buddha arrived at the place where Angulimal was watching from his secret hideout – a harmless monk quietly walking on the path. From his hideout Angulimal shouted, "Listen, don't come here! It is only because you are a sannyasin that I am warning you. Go back! I feel pity for you – watching you walk so quietly, walking so slowly. Go back, don't come any closer, because I am not used to feeling pity for anybody. I will kill you."

Buddha said to him, "I am also not used to feeling sorry for anybody. And when it's a challenge like this, how can a sannyasin back out? So I'm coming, and you should come out from where you are hiding."

Angulimal was really surprised: "This man must be mad!" He picked up his axe and went down. When he went close to Buddha he said, "You are inviting death unnecessarily."

Buddha said, "Before you kill me, just do one small thing. See that tree? – pluck four leaves from it."

Angulimal picked up his axe and chopped a branch off the tree and he said, "Here are four thousand leaves instead of four."

Buddha said, "Do one more thing. Before you kill me, re-connect that branch back to the tree."

And Angulimal said, "That will be difficult."

Buddha said, "Even a child can destroy something, but only someone who can make something come to life again is a real man, a powerful man. You are a weakling – you can

49

only destroy! Stop thinking of yourself as a strong man: you cannot even reconnect a small leaf back to the branch."

Angulimal thought seriously for a moment and said, "That is true. Is there really a way to rejoin the branch?"

Buddha said, "Yes! That is the path that I am on."

Angulimal thought, and his egoistic mind realized for the first time that there is no strength in killing; even a weak man can kill. So he said, "I am not weak, but what can I do?"

Buddha said, "Follow me."

Angulimal became a monk! He went into the village to beg for alms that very day, so everyone became afraid. They climbed up onto the roofs of their houses and started throwing stones at him. He fell down, bleeding; he was being hit by stones from everywhere. And Buddha went close to him and said, "Angulimal, *brahmin* Angulimal, get up! Today you have proved your courage. When their stones were hitting you your heart did not fill with anger. And even when your body started to bleed and you were wounded, your heart was filled with love for them. You have proved that you are a man. You have become a brahmin, one who has come to know the divine."

When Prasanjit heard of the change in Angulimal he went to see Buddha. He sat down and said, "I have heard that Angulimal has become a monk. Can I meet him?"

Buddha said, "The monk who is sitting next to me is Angulimal."

Hearing this, Prasanjit's hands and legs began to shake. This monk was still being called by the same name, and the fear that he felt also had not changed.

But Angulimal said, "Don't be afraid. That man is gone! The energy that was his has been transformed. Now I am on a different path. Now even if you killed me, I would not think ill of you."

People asked Buddha how such a cruel man could be so transformed. Buddha told them, "It is not a question of good or bad, it is only a question of transforming the energy."

Nobody in this world is a sinner and nobody is a saint. These are just pathways for energy. There is much energy stored inside our bodies, and this energy has to be used creatively.

So first, when an emotion arises, release it through your body in the form of any exercise. Second, learn to be creative. You are all without creativity.

Last night I was talking about how in the old days each village had a cobbler, and whenever somebody wore his shoes the cobbler would say with pride, "I have made them." It was an artist's pride. Another man would make wheels for the carts, and with pride he too would say, "They have been made by me."

In these times you have lost the pleasure from creating – there is not much left that is made by human hands. You don't create anything. The way the world is right now, soon there will be nothing left that has been made by human hands. And the joy one used to get from creating something has disappeared. If that is destroyed, what will happen to all this energy? – it will become destructive. Naturally, energy has to move in some direction, either towards destruction or towards creativity.

Learn to lead a creative life. Creativity means that you do something solely for the joy it gives you. You can sculpt, write a song, sing a song, play the sitar – it does not matter what you do, but do it only for pleasure and not as a profession. Do something in life which is only for pleasure, something which is not your profession. Then all the destructive energy will be transformed and will become creative.

I have asked you to redirect your emotions, and to give this ordinary life a creative direction. Don't worry, you can just make a garden around your house and love the plants and take pleasure in them. You don't have to do much – polish a stone and make a statue out of it! Every intelligent man needs to do something creative besides his means of livelihood. Someone who gives no time to creativity will be troubled, and he will ruin his own life.

You can write a small song – you don't have to do much. Go to a hospital and give flowers to the sick. If you see a beggar on the road, give him a hug. Do something creative which is only for your pleasure, in which you don't have to give anything and you don't have to take anything; the act itself is your joy.

So choose an activity in your life which is only for your pleasure. Direct all your energy towards it, and then there will be no destructive energy left. The more creative you are, the more your anger will disappear. Anger is the sign of an uncreative person. You carry so much energy within yourself – where will it go? It will come out through sex, through sexual desire. It has to come out somehow.

The reason that so many creative people, great sculptors, painters or poets, remained unmarried is that all their energy was being used for their creative process. Their energy was being transformed, being sublimated. Had it not been sublimated it would have been used in the least creative way, in the creation of children. Then the energy which could have been used to create something great, great poetry, great paintings, would have been used for reproduction. So it is very important to sublimate energy, to liberate it.

So remember this, that in order to totally purify the body you must try to live life creatively. Only a creative person can be religious – no one else can be religious.

I have mentioned some basic guidelines for the purification of the body, now a few more minor points. These first points are very basic. If they are taken care of, the minor things will automatically be taken care of.

One of the minor things that is very helpful for the purification of the body is nourishment. Your body is an absolutely physical mechanism: whatsoever you put into it will naturally affect it. If I drink alcohol the cells in my body will become unconscious – it is natural. And if my body is unconscious then it will have an effect on my mind. The body and the mind are not separate from each other, they are connected.

The body and the mind are not separate – they are together, a body-mind; it is psychosomatic. The mind and the body are one. The mind is the most subtle part of the body and the body is the most gross part of the mind. In other words, they are not two different things. That's why whatever happens in the body is echoed in the mind, and whatever happens in the mind has its effects on the body. If the mind is sick the body will not remain healthy for long, and if the body is sick then the mind will not be healthy for long. The message is passed between the two and has an effect on both. That's why people who learn how to keep the mind healthy automatically understand how to keep the body healthy. They don't have to work on it, they don't have to make any effort.

The body and the mind are connected. Whatever happens to the mind happens to the body. That's why you will have to be careful about your diet and what you eat.

First, you should not eat so much food that your body becomes lethargic; lethargy is unhealthy. Your food should also not make your body excited: excitement is unhealthy because excitement will create imbalances. You should eat enough so that the body does not waste away, because that will only create weakness. If energy is not produced then it will not be possible to progress towards higher consciousness. Your diet should create energy, but it should not be stimulating. Energy should be created, but you should not eat so much that it makes the body lethargic. If you have overeaten then all your energy will be used for digestion and the body will be filled with lethargy.

When the body is lethargic it means that all the energy is being used to digest your food. The rest of the body becomes lethargic. Lethargy is an indication that you have overeaten. After eating you should feel refreshed and energized, not lethargic. This is logical. When you are hungry, you eat; then you should feel refreshed because the fuel that you need to create energy has been supplied. Instead, you feel lazy. This laziness simply means that you have overeaten and now all your energy is being used in digesting that food. All the body's energy will be directed towards the stomach and the lack of energy in the rest of the body will make you feel lethargic.

So if the food energizes you, then it is right; if it does not stimulate you, then it is right; if it does not intoxicate you, then it is right. So remember these three things: if your diet is healthy it will not make you lethargic, if your diet is healthy then it will not stimulate you, if it is healthy it will not make you feel intoxicated. I don't think that you need any detailed explanation on this point. You can understand this and make the necessary adjustments.

Second among the minor points: exercise is absolutely important for the body, because all the elements that the body is made of expand with exercise. Exercise helps expansion. When you run, every cell, every living cell of your body expands. And when they expand you feel very healthy and when they are contracted you feel sick. When your lungs are filled with oxygen and all the carbon dioxide is thrown out, your blood pressure rises and the impurities are cleaned out. This is why in yoga the cleansing of the body, the total purification of the body is considered to be a vital necessity. So some exercise is good.

Excessive rest is harmful, excessive exercise is also harmful. This is why I am not asking you to do a lot of exercise, no excessive exercise: a little regular exercise will make you feel healthy. And don't rest too much, rest a little – rest only as much as you exercise.

In this century there is no place for exercise and rest. We are in a strange situation: we don't exercise and we also don't rest. What you call resting is not resting at all. You are lying down, tossing and turning – this is not rest. Rest is a long, deep sleep in which the whole body is sleeping, all its activities have slowed down and all the stress that it has been under is released.

Have you ever considered that when you get up in the

morning and you are not feeling refreshed and healthy, it affects your behavior? If you haven't slept and in the morning a beggar comes to you, it is unlikely that you will give him anything. But if you have had a good night's sleep, it is unlikely that you will refuse to give him something. That's why beggars come to your door in the morning, because in the morning it is easier for them to get something but not in the evening. This is perfectly logical. This is the reason why beggars come to beg in the morning and not in the evening; in the evening it is useless. By then you are so tired and the body is in a condition that you will probably not want to give anything. That's why they come in the morning. The sun has risen, you may have taken a bath, someone in the house has prayed and the beggar is standing outside. It will be very difficult to refuse him.

If the body has had a good rest your behavior will change accordingly. That's why food and rest have always been taken in relation to each other. Your diet should be related to your lifestyle. If there is purity in both, then you can have immense movement in your life, and it will be easier for you to enter the inner world.

The same way that you need to understand how to exercise, some understanding is also needed about how to rest. In order to rest you need to know how to relax your body. You will understand this when we meditate tonight. When you rest after the meditation you will really be resting.

It is possible that there are friends here who are not able to do regular exercise, who can't go to the forest, who will not be able to climb the mountains. For them I will suggest another meditation.

In the morning, after having a bath, they should lie on the

bed in a closed room for fifteen minutes and imagine that they are climbing a mountain or that they are jogging. Just imagine and don't do anything. The old people can't actually go to the mountains. Then lie down in a closed room with your eyes closed and picture yourself climbing a mountain or running. The sun is shining and you are running; you have started breathing heavily. You will be surprised to notice that you will actually start breathing heavily. And if your imagination is powerful enough, then in fifteen minutes you will find that you have had the experience of actually being outdoors. In fifteen minutes you will feel as fresh as if you have just exercised. It is not needed for you to actually exercise because the cells in the body that you would exercise are being aroused. In other words, they will come to the state that they would be in if you had actually exercised.

Have you ever wondered why when you become afraid in a dream and you wake up, your heart is still beating fast? The fear was in the dream, it was unreal – then why is the heart beating so fast? Why is it beating fast even after you are awake? The heart is beating fast because it does not know whether the fear was in a dream or whether it was in reality. The heart just knows that there is fear. Just like this, if you imagine that you are exercising it will be as helpful as if you had really exercised; there is no difference. That's why the people who were knowledgeable in these things created these techniques. If you put them into a small cell it would not harm their health because they would rest for fifteen minutes and do their exercise in this way.

Try this. Whoever is unable to go out can use this technique as well as the meditation for sleep which is to be done at night. You can do them both just before sleeping.

The body can be purified in this way. And if the body is pure, this will itself be a great joy, and in this joy you can go deeper inside. This is the first step.

There are two other steps: purification of thought and purification of the soul. I will explain these.

On the periphery there are three steps: body purification, mind purification and emotional purification; and then there are three steps for the center: bodilessness, thoughtlessness and freedom from emotions. When these six stages are completed, *samadhi* happens. So, step by step, we will talk about them during these three days and that will be enough. You will think about them, understand them and try them, because whatever I talk about is for you to experiment with. The meaning will only be clear to you if you try it; otherwise my talks will not reveal any secrets to you.

Now we will do the morning meditation. About the morning meditation, I would like to say that the first step will be the same as what we practiced last night: making a resolution. We will make the resolution five times. After this we will rest for two minutes, taking deep breaths. Then we will meditate silently for a while.

First we make the resolution, then we rest, and the last step is meditation. These will be the three steps of the meditation for the mornings. The resolution will be the same as what I suggested last night: breathe deeply, and while the air is coming in keep the thought in mind, "I'm going to make a conscious effort to enter into meditation. I will experience meditation." Keep this thought going continuously while the breath is coming in and the lungs are filling up. Fill the lungs as much as you can, then hold your breath for one second, for two seconds, as long as you can. When you breathe in take in as much air as you can, then hold your breath for a while. In yoga these exercises are called *purak, rumbhak, rechak.* Inhale and hold it at the same time as you make your resolution, let it ring through your mind; then exhale and let the thought keep ringing in your mind; then wait, letting the thought continue to ring through your mind. In this way the resolution will reach to your unconscious mind, deep inside. Your whole being will know that you have made the decision to enter into meditation. Then your whole being will help you; otherwise you will just wander around here and there will be no change.

So first make the resolution, then focus on the emotional state. After you have made the resolution, for two minutes you should invoke the feelings of hope and joy that I spoke about yesterday. For two minutes consider your body to be in a very healthy condition; imagine that you are experiencing great joy, that every cell of your body is alive and you are filled with hope. Things will happen – just make the decision. Then feel that there is peace all around you, that there is great bliss inside you, that you are full of hope and every cell of your body is alive and joyous. After this we will do the morning meditation.

During the morning meditation keep your back straight, be relaxed and still. All movement of the body has to stop and your back has to be straight. Close your eyes and take slow breaths, very slowly breathing in and slowly breathing out. Watch your breath. Keep your eyes closed and watch your breath going in and coming out.

There are two ways to watch your breath: one is to watch

your abdomen, where your stomach moves up and down; and the second is near the nose, where the breath goes out. Do whichever is easier for you. Most people find it easier to watch the nose. When the air moves in it touches the nose and when it moves out it again touches the nose. Watch that spot where the breath touches, going in, coming out. Anyone who has tried to concentrate on the navel before will find it easier to watch the navel. He should watch the navel, the belly rising and falling. Focus where you feel most comfortable. Watch your breath for ten minutes.

Now we will settle down for the morning meditation. Sit apart from each other. Sit far enough apart so that you don't touch or hear anyone else.

THE PATH OF MEDITATION
finding quality in life

Chapter 3

My Beloved Ones,

*f*IRST THERE IS a question: *If a seeker finds a ray of light, how should he take care of this experience?*

As I said this morning, whatever feelings of joy, of peace, of happiness you experience, they are to be carried inside you continuously, for twenty-four hours a day. How will you do this? There are two ways: one way is to remember and re-create this particular state of consciousness which you have experienced while you were meditating.

For example, during meditation you breathe slowly, so during the day whenever you find the time, when you are not doing anything in particular, slow down your breathing and keep your attention on the spot under the nose where the breath enters. Remembering these feelings, imagine your-self to be feeling happy, joyous, silent and nourished. Bring these feelings back. Whenever you remember – going to bed, waking up, walking on the street, wherever you may be – bring these feelings back. The result will be that many times during the day this remembrance will strike at something inside you. And a time will come when you will not have to make any special effort to remember; it will be with you constantly, just like your breathing.

So first, you have to continuously remember these feel-ings within yourself, whenever the thought comes to you.

For example, while lying in bed remember the state you were in while you were meditating. When you go for a walk, when you see the moonlight in the night, when you sit under a tree and there is no one around, when you are alone in your room, remember the feelings. Traveling on a bus or traveling in a train, sitting alone, close your eyes and remember these feelings. Even during the day when you are busy with your work, even in your office, get up for a few minutes and go to a window, take a few deep breaths and try to remember that state of being.

If you do this even for ten or fifteen times a day, remembering for a minute or two, it will become more and more continuous. Slowly you will find that there is no need to remember – it will remain with you. So this is one way: by carrying whatsoever you experience in meditation in your thoughts and letting it enter into your consciousness.

The second way is what I have already suggested to you, that when you go to bed at night you make your resolution. The way to make your resolution stronger is also a way to make your state of meditation a continuous one. When you have had an experience of meditation, that night when you go to bed, do the same: recall inside whatsoever you have experienced during meditation and the same experience will be with you for twenty-four hours a day.

The exercise that I have given you to make your resolution of throwing your breath out and making the resolution and then taking the breath in and making the resolution…when you experience a state of silence, then using the same procedure, bring the thought to mind that whatever you feel during meditation will be with you all the time like an inner current. By repeating this thought you will find the feeling of meditation without any effort. It will be more beneficial if the two things are done simultaneously. Later on, when we talk about the purification of thoughts and emotions, we will be able to discuss this more deeply. But you can experiment with both these exercises.

During the course of twenty-four hours you have a lot of free time on your hands when you don't have anything worthwhile to do. If this free time can be used to remember these moments of meditation, it can make a tremendous difference. Look at it this way: two years ago someone insulted you, or you experienced a tragic incident – if today you were to try to remember this incident you will be surprised to notice that as you remember the whole incident your body and your mind will slowly come to the same state they were in when you actually went through the experience two years ago. If two years ago you were insulted by someone and today you were to try to remember this incident, how it felt and how you were insulted, you will be surprised to see that your body and your mind will experience the same state they were in then, as if you are again being insulted.

Everything is being collected in your consciousness and it does not disappear. Whatever you have experienced is stored. If you bring back these memories you can experience the same things again and you can go through the same emotions again. Nothing is erased from the human mind.

So if while you were meditating today you felt good, it is essential that you remember this experience at least five to ten times during the day. In this way the memory of this experience will go deeper into your consciousness, and by remembering it again and again it will become a permanent part of your consciousness. So in answer to the question that has been asked, this is how it can be done. And it is important that you do it.

✳Very often people make the mistake of remembering only what is negative and forgetting everything that is positive. The basic mistake that people make is that they remember all that is worthless, negative, and they forget all that has any real value. Rarely will you remember the moment when you were full of love; you will rarely remember those moments when your body felt totally alive. You rarely remember those moments when you felt silent. But you will always remember the moments when you were angry and upset, the moments when you were insulted and when you took revenge on somebody. You will always remember the times when you were hurt but rarely the times which were nourishing to you. And it is very important for you to remember these nourishing moments.

To remember them continually will help you in two ways. Most importantly, remembering these moments will create a possibility for them to happen again. If someone constantly remembers the negative things, it is extremely likely that he will go through the same kind of experiences again. If someone constantly remembers sad things it is very likely that he will be sad again, because he will develop an inclination towards these things and these incidents will keep repeating in his life. All these feelings become stored inside you, and it becomes more and more easy for these emotions to repeat themselves again and again.

Try to observe in yourself the kind of emotions that you have a tendency to remember. We all have memories. What kind of experiences do you tend to remember? And remember also that whatever memories you have of the past, you are planting these as seeds for the future and you will reap the same experiences in the future. Your memories of the past pave the way for the future.

Consciously forget everything that is worthless – it does not have any value! And if you do remember such things, then stop yourself and ask those memories to go away. They are of no use to you. Forget all the thorns and remember the flowers. There may be many thorns, but there are also flowers around. If you remember the flowers the thorns in your life will disappear and your life will be filled with flowers. If you remember the thorns, it is possible that the flowers in your life will disappear and you will be left with only the thorns.

What we become depends on what memories we nourish because what we remember becomes part of us. When we think of something all the time, this thought brings about a change in us and it becomes our whole life. Hence, remember everything that you think is good and pure, whatever you think is important. And in life...nobody's life is so miserable that there have been no moments of peace, happiness, beauty, love. And if remembering these moments gives you some strength, then it is possible that even when you are surrounded by darkness, the light inside you will be so strong that you will not see this darkness. It is possible that there may be sorrow all around you but you are carrying this experience of love, of beauty, of silence within you, so you don't see all the sorrow. It is possible that in spite of being surrounded by thorns, a person may feel that he is surrounded by flowers. But the opposite of this is also possible – it all depends on you.

It depends on the individual to what heights he wants to

reach. It depends on us whether we live in heaven or in hell. Heaven and hell are not geographical places, they are subjective, psychological states. Most of you are in hell many times in a day and many times you are in heaven. But most of you are in hell for the major part of the day, and some of you even forget the way back to heaven.

But there are also people who are in heaven for twenty-four hours a day. There are people on this same planet who are living in heaven. You too can be one of them. There is nothing to stop you. Just understand some basic, scientific principles.

I remember a story....

Buddha had a disciple called Purna. He had been initiated and had become self-realized. Purna said, "Now I want to leave and spread your message to all the people who need it."

Buddha said, "I can give you permission to leave, but I have to ask you one thing first: where do you want to go?"

There was a small region in Bihar called Sukha. Purna said, "I will go to Sukha. Until now no monk has ever visited this area, and the people of this region have never heard your message."

Buddha said, "There is a reason why no one has ever been there. The people there are very bad. It is possible that if you go there they will insult you. Then what will your response be?"

And Purna said, "I will thank them. I will thank them because even if they abuse me, at least they did not hit me – they could have hit me."

Buddha said, "It is possible that one of them may hit you;

then what will your response be?"

He replied, "I will thank him because even if he hits me, at least he did not kill me. He could have killed me."

Buddha said, "I want to ask you one last question. It is possible that someone will kill you. Then what will your response be?"

Purna said, "I will thank him for releasing me from this life in which I could have gone astray."

And Buddha said, "In that case, you can go anywhere! Now wherever you go, for you, everyone will be a part of your family. Because when a person's heart is so full, at such a peak, nothing on this earth can hurt him."

Yesterday I was talking to someone on the way here about Mahavira. It is said about Mahavira, although it may seem to be untrue, that if he was walking on the road even the thorns that were sticking up would turn over. This seems to be fictitious. What does it matter to the thorns who is walking over them? Of what interest is it to a thorn whether it is Mahavira or somebody else walking over them? And how can a thorn turn over? I have also heard it said about Mohammed that when he walked in the hot Arabian deserts, a cloud would appear above him to shade him from the sun. This seems to be absolute fiction. What does it matter to a cloud who is walking below it, whether it is Mohammed or someone else? How is it possible?

But I tell you, it is all true. It is not that thorns turn over or that clouds appear, but these stories are revealing something to us. People have tried to express some truth through them. Through them something very lovely is being conveyed

– that no thorns can hurt someone whose own heart has become free of thorns. And for someone who carries no burning passion in his heart, the whole earth is covered with a cloud of shade and he is never exposed to the scorching sun. And this is absolutely true.

Whatever your state of consciousness is, your life will also have the same quality. It is a wonder that when someone makes an effort to purify himself the whole world becomes a friendly place to him; and when someone is full of love the whole world showers its love on him. And this is the eternal truth: that someone who is full of hatred will receive hatred in return. Whatever we put out, all comes back to us. There is no other way, no alternative.

So for twenty-four hours a day try to remember those moments in your life that have been magical and sacred. Recall those few moments and try to make them the foundation of your life. And try to forget even the long periods of pain, sorrow, hatred and violence; they don't have any value. Let them fade away. Just like the dry leaves fall from the trees, let go of all that is of no value and consciously go on gathering all that is meaningful and alive. This process should go on continuously. There should be a flow of pure, beautiful thoughts in your mind, full of love and happiness.

Then, step by step, you will find that the things you remember seem to happen more often and that what you are always longing for will start appearing all around you. And then the world will appear in a totally different light. The same people will appear different: the same eyes, the same flower and the same stone will appear to have a different meaning...something we have never even thought of because we are engrossed in a totally different world.

So as I have said, remember what you have experienced in meditation – the brightness, a ray, a little peace. Look after the small experiences that you have had just like a mother looks after her child. If you don't look after them they will die. The more valuable a thing is, the more need there is to take care of it. Animals also have children but they don't need much care; the less developed the animal, the less need there is to care for them. They take care of themselves. But on the ladder of evolution you will find that if a human child is not looked after properly it will not survive.

The higher the state of consciousness, the more protection is needed. The more precious the experience, the more care it requires. So even if you have only small experiences, look after them carefully.

You have asked how to take care of them? If I were to give you a few diamonds, how would you take care of them? If you were to find a valuable treasure, how would you take care of it? How would you keep it safe? Where would you keep it? You would want to hide it away; you would want to keep it close to your heart.

A beggar was dying in the hospital. When the priest visited him the doctors told him that he was going to die. So the priest went to him for his last rites. He told the beggar, "Fold your hands together."

But the beggar said, "Forgive me, but I cannot open one hand."

He was about to die and he could not open one of his hands. And a few moments later, he died. His hands were

70

opened and they found a few dirty coins which he had collected. He had been holding these in his fist…a few dirty coins! He knew that he was going to die but he kept his hand closed.

You know how to take care of ordinary coins – everyone knows that – but you don't know how to look after that which is the most valuable. And you are like this beggar, with your fists closed. And when the time comes for your fists to be opened there will be nothing in them except for a few dirty coins.

Protect these experiences…they are the real coins. They may have inspired you, they may have given you fresh juice, they may have transformed something in you; something new may have been triggered in you, a longing for the ultimate may have arisen in you. So take care of them. I have explained both methods. If you go on experimenting with them you will understand.

Another friend has asked: *Is sex a creative energy? How can the relationship between a husband and a wife be made creative?*

This is an important question. There are very few people for whom this question will not be important.

There are only two types of people in this world: one type is the people who are suffering because of sex, and the other is the people who have transformed their sexual energy into love.

You will be surprised to know that sex and love are two opposite things. As love grows sex becomes less, and if love becomes less sex becomes more. The more loving you are the less sexual you will be; and if you are totally filled with love there will be nothing sexual inside you. But if there is no love, inside you everything will be sexual.

The transformation, the sublimation of sexual energy can only happen through love. This is why it is useless to try to suppress sex to get free of it. If you suppress it you can go insane. Of all the insane people in the world, ninety-nine out of a hundred have tried to repress their sexual energy. And you may be aware that as civilization has developed, insanity has increased because civilized society suppresses sex more than anything else.

Everyone suppresses his sexual energy. And that suppressed sexual energy creates insanity; it creates mental illnesses. Any attempt to suppress your sexual energy is in itself madness. Many of the so-called saints are in fact insane. And the only reason for this is that they have constantly tried to suppress their sexual energy; they don't know that sex should not be suppressed..

If the doors to love are opened, the energy that was flowing through sex will be transformed through the light of love. What had been the flames of passion will become the light of love. So let this love expand. Love is the creative use of sex.

Fill your life with love. But you will say, "We always love." And I tell you, you rarely love. You might be longing for love…and there is a vast difference between the two. To love and to need love are two very different things. Most of us remain like children all our lives because everyone is looking for love. To love is a very mysterious thing; to long for love is a very childish thing. Small children want love; when the mother gives them love they grow. They want love from

72

others also and the family loves them. Then when they grow older, if they are husbands they want love from their wives, if they are wives they want love from their husbands. And whoever wants love suffers because love cannot be asked for, love can only be given. In wanting there is no certainty that you will get it. And if the person from whom you expect love also expects love from you, it is a problem. It will be like two beggars meeting and begging together. All over the world there are marital problems between husbands and wives, and the only reason for this is that both expect love from each other but are unable to give love.

Think about this a little – your constant need for love. You want someone to love you, and if someone loves you you feel good. But what you don't know is that the other loves you only because he wants you to love him. It is just like someone throwing bait to fish: he does not throw it for the fish to eat, he throws it to catch the fish. He does not want to give it to the fish, he only does it because he wants the fish. All the people that you see in love around you are only throwing bait to get love. They will throw the bait for a while, until the other person starts feeling that there is a possibility of getting love from this person. Then he too will start showing some love until eventually they realize that both of them are beggars. They have made a mistake: each had thought the other was an emperor. And in time each one realizes that he is not getting any love from the other, and that's when the friction starts.

That's why married life is thought to be hell, because you all want love but you don't know how to give it. This is the basic cause of all fights. As long as what I am saying does not happen, the relationship between a husband and a wife will never be harmonious, no matter what adjustments you make, no matter what kind of marriage you have, no matter what rules society makes. The only way to make it better is if you realize that love can only be given and not asked for. It can *only* be given. Whatever you receive is a blessing, it is not a reward for loving. Love is to be given and whatever you receive is just a blessing, it is not a reward. And even if you don't receive anything you are always happy that you were able to give.

If the husband and wife were to start giving love instead of asking for it, life could become heaven for them. And this world is so mysterious that if they love more and stop asking for it, they will receive more love and experience this mystery. And the more they love the less they will be involved in sex.

Gandhi was visiting Sri Lanka with his wife, Kasturba. When Gandhi told the person who was to introduce him at the first function that Ba, his wife, was also with him, this person thought that Gandhi meant his mother. From the word *ba,* mother, he had taken it to mean that Gandhi's mother had also come with him. So introducing Gandhi he said, "It is a great privilege to have Gandhi here, and his mother is also here."

Ba was a bit surprised. Gandhi's secretary was also present, and he was afraid that he had made a mistake because he should have told the man who it was that was with Gandhi. He was afraid that Gandhi would be angry with him and feel insulted.

But what Gandhi said was quite amazing. He said, "The person who introduced me has by mistake said something true about me, because for a few years Ba has stopped being my wife and she has now become my mother."

A true sannyasin is the one whose wife one day becomes his mother, and not the one who leaves his wife and runs away. A true sannyasin is the one whose husband one day becomes her son.

There is a beautiful saying of the old sages. In the old days a sage would give the blessing, "May you be blessed with ten sons and may your husband become your eleventh son." This is strange. It was the blessing that was given to the bride at the time of her marriage: may you be blessed with ten sons and may your husband become your eleventh son. These were wonderful people, with wonderful ways of thinking. And there was also a profound meaning behind it.

If the love between a husband and wife grows they will no longer be husband and wife: their relationship will change and there will be less sex between them. Their relationship will change into love. As long as there is sex, there is exploitation. Sex is exploitation – and how can you exploit the person you love? Sex is the most degrading and the most exploitive use of a living being. If you love someone how can you exploit them in such a way? How can you use a living being in such a way? If you love someone, as your love goes deeper the exploitation will disappear. And if your love disappears the exploitation will again increase.

This is why I would like to say to the person who has asked about how to make sex a creative energy that sex is a very mysterious energy. There is no energy on the planet as powerful as sexual energy. Most of man's focus is on sex. Ninety percent of his life is based in the sex center, it is not based in the divine. There are very few people whose lives revolve around the divine. Most people are revolving around and living their lives through the sex center. Sex is the greatest energy. And if understood rightly, you will see that there is no other energy which motivates man as much as sex. But this sexual energy itself can be transformed into love. And this same energy, if transformed, can become the path to enlightenment.

So it is worth noting that religion is deeply connected with sex – not with the repression of sex, as is commonly understood, but with the transformation of sex. Religion is not about the repression of sex. Celibacy is not the opposite of sex, it is the transformation of sex. The energy of sex itself is transformed into the divine energy. The energy which was flowing downwards, which was descending, starts moving upwards. If the sexual energy is rising upwards it will help you to attain the ultimate state of consciousness. And if this energy is moving downwards it leads only to a mundane existence. But this energy can be transformed through love.

Learn how to love. Learn the meaning of love. Later on, when we talk about emotions, then you will clearly understand the meaning of love. For now I will say only this much.

One friend has asked: *Why don't the sages work together as a group?*

It is a very good question: why don't the sages, those who have known truth, work together as a group? I would like to say that the sages have always worked together. And I would like to add that not only have those sages who are alive worked together, but even the sages who died twenty-five centuries ago are helping those who are alive. So it is not that only contemporary sages are working together. On the contrary, when considered historically, traditionally, they have always been working together.

If what I am saying is truth, it is because I have the support of Buddha, Mahavira, Krishna and Christ. If what I am saying is truth, then their words are also merged in mine. And if there is any strength in my words it is not only my own but the strength of all of those who have used these word in the past.

But the people who are not sages will never work together. And there are many so-called sages who are not real religious people, they only appear to be. Only unscrupulous people can work together with them, not the sages that I have just mentioned.

Why is it that these people cannot work together? – because they have not become saints by dissolving their egos. Their sainthood is also a way to feed their egos. And where there is ego no meeting is possible because ego always wants to be on top.

I was at a conference to which many religious figures had been invited. It was a big event, many important religious leaders had been invited. I will not name them because someone might feel hurt, but many of India's important people were there. The person who organized the event wanted all the guests to sit together on the stage and to address the audience from there. But one particular religious leader was not willing to sit with everyone else, and he sent a message asking him, "Who will be sitting above and who will sit below?" And he said, "I will sit above. I cannot sit beneath anyone."

A person who speaks up for himself is at least straightforward, but someone who sends a message like this is complicated and very cunning. This man sent a message that he could not sit with everyone else. The big platform that had been organized was of no use, so every speaker had to sit alone on the stage to address the gathering. And the stage was big enough to seat a hundred people!

But how could a hundred religious leaders sit together? Amongst them there were a few *shankaracharyas* who could not sit anywhere except on their thrones. And if they could not sit on the floor, how could the other religious leaders sit on the floor next to their thrones? It makes one wonder if people like this think that some chairs are greater than others, and if they still feel that you are measured by the seat you take, by how high or how low your seat is. It simply shows what they consider to be important.

Two religious leaders cannot meet because the problem will arise as to who will be the first to fold his hands in greeting, because the one who greets first in some way becomes lower than the other. It is surprising, because the person who folds his hands first is really the superior one. But these religious heads think that the one who folds his hands first becomes inferior.

I was at the meeting of an important religious man. A very important politician was also attending the meeting. The religious man was seated on a raised platform and the rest of us were seated below. The meeting began, and the politician said, "I would first like to ask why we are all seated down here and you are sitting up there? If you were going to give a speech it would be acceptable. But this is a meeting, there will be a discussion, and you are sitting so high that it will be impossible to discuss anything. Kindly come down."

But the religious man would not come down. Then the politician asked, "If you cannot come down, if there is a particular reason, then explain it to us."

But he could not answer, he was afraid. Instead, one of his disciples said, "It has always been the tradition that he should sit on a higher level."

The politician said, "He may be your guru, but he is not our guru." And he added, "And we folded our hands to greet you but you did not fold your hands in return – you gave us your blessings! Consider this: if another religious man had come to meet you and you had given him your blessings, there would have been a fight. You also should have folded your hands."

And the reply was, "He cannot fold his hands because that is not the tradition."

The situation became so ugly that any discussion was impossible. I told this religious man, "I would like to ask for permission to say a few words to this politician." He gave me his permission. He wanted the incident to be finished with so that the meeting could proceed. Things had come to a standstill. I asked this politician, "Why is it that the first thing you noticed was that he is sitting higher than everyone else?" And I said, "And may I ask, did you notice that he is sitting higher up or did you notice that you have been made to sit below? – because it is also possible that you could be asked to sit higher up; then I don't think you would have raised the question. If we all were sitting below and if you were sitting with him on the platform, I don't think you would have raised the question. The problem is not created by his sitting higher up, the problem for you is that you are sitting below."

That politician looked at me. He was in a position of great power at the time, and one of the most prominent people in India. He looked at me very attentively, he was a very sincere man. He said, "I accept that. Nobody has ever said this to me. Yes, this is being very egoistic."

The religious man was very pleased, and when we were leaving he put his arm around my shoulder and said, "You gave a very good reply to him." I told him, "That answer was not only for him, it was also meant for you." And I said to him, "I was sorry to see that he is more honest than you, and that you showed no honesty at all. He accepted that it is his ego, but you did not even acknowledge it; instead you fed your ego with the help of my answer!"

Religious men of this type cannot work together. Their whole work is based on criticizing others. Their whole effort is based on opposing someone. If there are no enemies, they cannot work at all. All their efforts are based on opposing and hating others. All the religious men who follow these traditions, these religions, can only be called ignorant, because the first attribute of a genuine sage is that he no longer belongs to any religion. The first mark of a sage is that he is no longer bound by any limits or traditions. He will not have any restrictions, he will belong to everyone. And his first attribute will be that his ego will have dissolved and his pride will have disappeared. But these are ways to boost the ego, to give it nourishment.

Remember this: the ego is satisfied with much wealth, the ego can be satisfied if you have gone through much suffering, and if you acquire much knowledge this will also boost your . ego. If I renounce the world I am boosting my ego. And those whose egos are satisfied can never work together. Ego is the only dividing factor and egolessness is the only joining factor. So where there is egolessness, there is togetherness.

Once a Mohammedan fakir called Farid was passing by the village where Kabir lived. He was traveling with a few of his disciples. His disciples told him, "It is very fortunate that we will be passing by the house where Kabir lives. Let us stay at his house for a few days. It would give us immense joy if the two of you had a dialogue. If the two of you were to meet and have a dialogue it would be of great benefit to us."

Farid said, "Yes, we will stop and meet, but there may not be a dialogue."

They asked him, "Why?"

He said, "We will stop there. I will meet him but we may not talk."

When Kabir's disciples heard they said, "Farid is going to pass by here – let us receive him. It will be a happy occasion. For two days the two of you can talk."

And Kabir said, "We should definitely meet. Everyone will be very happy."

Farid was welcomed. Farid and Kabir embraced each other. Their eyes were filled with tears of joy but no dialogue happened between them. They parted, and the disciples were very disappointed. As they were parting the disciples said, "But you have not said anything!"

And they replied, "What can be said? What he knows, I also know."

Farid said, "What I know, Kabir also knows, so what can we talk about? We are not even two people who can talk – at some level we are one. On that level words are unnecessary."

Among sages a dialogue is not possible. Even to speak creates a duality. At some level, the eternal work of all the sages is the same. There is no question of any duality on that level. No matter where they are born, what community they belong to, whatever their way of life may be, there is still no duality among them. But with those who are not sages it is only natural that there should be differences between them. That is why – and remember this – there are no differences between sages. And if there are differences, then consider it to be a sign that those people are not sages.

A friend has asked: *What is your final aim or objective?*

He has asked me what my aim is. I don't have any aim. And it will be good to understand why I have no aim, no objective.

There are two kinds of actions in life. One type of action is motivated by desire, there is a goal behind it. Then there is another type of action which is motivated by love, by compassion – there is no objective behind it. If you ask a mother, "What is the objective behind the love you give your child?" what will she say? She will say, "I don't know about any objective. I just love, and there is joy in just loving." It is not that you love today and receive the joy tomorrow. Your love itself is the joy.

But there is also a type of action which is motivated by desire. Right now I am talking to you. I could be speaking because I will get something out of it. The reward could be in the form of money, fame, respect, prestige – it could be in any form. I may be talking because I will get something in return; then it would be motivated by desire.

But I am speaking only because I cannot stop myself from speaking. Something has happened inside and it wants to be shared. My talking is like a flower that has bloomed and is spreading its fragrance all around. If you ask a flower, "What is the goal?"…there is no goal behind it.

Some acts arise out of desire; then there is a goal behind them. There are some actions which are motivated by compassion; then there is no goal hidden behind them. This is why when an act arises out of a desire it creates a bondage. But acts that arise out of compassion don't create any bondage. Any act which has a goal creates bondage and one which has no goal does not create bondage.

And you will be surprised to know that you cannot do wrong unless you have a goal. It is a strange thing: there is always a goal in sin; there is no goal when you do a good deed. And if there is a goal in a good deed, it must be a sin in disguise. There is always a goal in sin. Without a goal there would be no sin. Even with a goal it is difficult to sin, so without a goal it is impossible. I cannot kill you without a reason – why would I kill you? Sin cannot exist without a reason. Because a sin cannot be committed through compassion a sin will always be filled with desire, and desire always implies a goal. There will be an expectation of something in return. But it is possible to act without having any expectations.

After Mahavira became enlightened he continued to work for some forty more years. Why did he do this? He had worked for so many years, so why did he not stop? For so many years he had been on the move all the time; he was so active: he would eat, go here, go there, give talks, give discourses. For forty to forty-five years he was continually working. Wasn't he satisfied? After Buddha became enlightened he also kept working for forty more years. Why did he not stop? – because in this activity there was no goal. Neither did Buddha or Mahavira have any goal, it was simply out of their compassion.

I often wonder why I go on talking to you. What is the purpose behind it? I don't find a purpose even when I look for one, except that I can see something and there is a need for me to speak about it. In fact, only the person who still has some violence in him would be able to keep quiet about it.

Why would this be violent?... This morning I told you a story: if I see a snake in your hand and without saying anything I start walking on my way thinking that it has nothing to do with me, it would only be possible if there is violence, cruelty inside me. Otherwise I would tell you, "It is a snake! Throw it away!"

And if someone were to ask me, "Why are you saying that it is a snake, to throw it away? Why does it matter to you?" I would answer, "It doesn't matter to me at all, except that it is not possible for my inner consciousness to keep quiet in a situation like this."

The motivation is not because of any external thing, since there is no goal behind it. The motivation stems from an inner consciousness where there is no expectation. You will be surprised that whenever there is a goal you are externally motivated, and when there is no goal your motivation comes from deep inside. That is, if there is anything which attracts you there is a goal. There are things which pull us from inside, but then there is no goal.

Love and compassion are always without an objective, desires and wants are always goal-oriented. This is why it is better to say that desire pulls, pulls from the outside. If I tie a rope around you and pull you, this is pulling. Desire pulls you as if you have been tied with a rope and are being pulled by it. That is why our religious scriptures call someone who has desires a *pashu*. The word 'pashu' means an animal that is tied with a rope, that is tied to something else and is being pulled by it. But in the scriptures the word 'pashu' does not mean an animal; 'pashu' is used to indicate a person who is tied with a rope and is being pulled by it. As long as you are pulled by a goal there is desire, and as long as that exists you are tied with a rope like the animals. You are not free. Freedom is the opposite of pashu, of being tied and dragged along. Freedom means to not be dragged along in any kind of bondage, but to move from a flow that comes from within oneself.

I don't have any goal. This is why if I die this moment I would not feel even for a second that I have left something undone. If I died right now, sitting here, I would not think even for a moment that what I have to say has been left unsaid because there is no motive behind it, it is not a question of completing something. As long as I am alive the work is being done, and when I die the work ends. Since there is no motive behind it nothing is left incomplete.

I have no motive, there is only an inspiration from within. There is an inner compulsion and whatever happens, happens because of it. In India we say that such a person has surrendered himself to existence. Now all his acts will be God's wish: he does not have a motive of his own. It is right to say that all his acts are God's wish, because he has surrendered his life to the ultimate. Now all that happens is the responsibility of the ultimate, he himself is not responsible.

You have asked a good question. I would like to say that life should be free of desire and pain. Create a life in which there are no motives and an inspiration will emerge from within you. Make your life such that you have no desire to gain anything but you have a desire to give. What I call love means that you don't ask for it, you just give it. And there is no goal in love except giving. What I call love I also call compassion. So you can say that there is no goal except to love. And love does not have a goal because love itself is the goal.

There is one last question about anger: *When one becomes angry it produces adverse results and has an effect on the whole body. In this state, what blockages can happen in the body?*

This morning when I spoke to you, I told you that anger is just an example. All emotions are energies, and if these energies are not used creatively they will disturb some part of the body, some part of the mind. The energy has to be used. The energy which is inside without being used will create certain blocks. These blocks will become a disease, like a tumor. Do you understand? It is not just with anger – if there is love within me to give and I am not able to give this love to someone, it can create a blockage within me. If there is anger inside me and I am not able to express it, it can create a blockage within me. If there is fear inside and I am not able to show it, fear can become a blockage. All emotional states create energy within and this energy needs to be released.

This release can be of two types. One is a *via negativa*. For example, someone is angry, so the negative way for this person would be to go and throw some stones at someone else, beat someone up with a stick or verbally attack him. This way is negative, because his energy is used up but he does not benefit from it. The only fruits he will harvest will be when the person he has attacked verbally retaliates with double the force. The person at whom he threw stones will also get angry. He is just like the first person: he will also use a negative mode to express his anger. He will also pick up a stick.

If you throw a stone at someone then he will throw a bigger stone back at you. If anger is used in a negative way then it will create more anger and the energy will be wasted. Again anger will be created, and because of the negative habit more anger will again be generated. Again energy will be wasted and again because of the other person's reaction there will be anger. There will be an unlimited amount of anger in which energy will only be wasted, and it never ends.

Anger will stop only if you use it in a positive way, in a creative way. That is why Mahavira has said, "A person who hates will receive hate in return. A person who shows anger receives anger. A person who has evil thoughts will receive the same in return." There is no end to it, and in the end energy will only be wasted.

Suppose I am angry – in return you are angry; again I get angry with you and again in reaction you get angry with me. What will be the result of all this? Every time I get angry it will weaken me and it will use up all my energy. This is why society has made it a practice not to show anger. This is the reason why society discourages you from showing your anger towards another person. It is a good rule, and because of this anger will not be expressed and it will not multiply. But that energy will still be there inside me. Then what will happen to it?

Have you observed the eyes of an animal? Even the most ferocious of animals has eyes that are softer than yours. The eyes of a wild animal are softer than the eyes of a human being. Why is this so? – it is because there is no suppressed energy in them. When an animal is angry it will express it: it roars, cries out, attacks, and it releases the anger. It is not civilized. Whatever impulse it has will be expressed.

What is the reason for the softness that you see in the eyes of children? They express whatever they feel; their energies don't create any blockages. When they are angry they express their anger, when they are jealous they show it, when they want to snatch a toy from another child they do it. There is no suppression in the lives of children – that's why they are so innocent.

There is suppression in your life and that is where the complications begin. A block in the energy reflects an inner complexity – something happens inside but you show something else outside. Then where will the energy which is not released go? It will become an energy-block.

What I mean by an energy-block is that it is stuck in your mind or in your body like a knot. It is just like in a river when part of the water starts to freeze and pieces of ice float in the river. As the pieces become bigger and bigger, the flow of the river is obstructed more and more. If all the water freezes the river will stop flowing altogether. So you are like a river which has blocks of ice floating in it. It is necessary to melt this ice.

These energy-blocks are like blocks of ice floating in your lifestream. The repressed impulses of hatred, of anger and of sex have become like big blocks of ice inside you. Now they will not let the flow of life go on. Some people's lives have become totally frozen, there is no flow at all. It is absolutely necessary to melt the ice, and to melt the ice a creative method should be used. I have explained two creative ways to do this: one is to let go of the old blocked impulses and the other is to make a creative use of new impulses.

If you look at little children they have so much passion, so much energy inside them. If you leave them in the house they will touch this and bang that, break this and crush that. And you tell them, "Don't do this, don't do that." You tell them not to do something but you don't tell them what to do instead. And you don't know what a child is doing when he breaks a glass. The energy inside him needs some outlet. Now there is no other way, so he picks up a glass and by banging that glass his energy finds an outlet, it is released. But then you tell him, "Don't break the glass," and he stops banging the glass. He goes outside, and now he wants to pick the flowers. You say, "Don't touch the flowers." He cannot even touch the flowers! He goes inside and picks up a book and you say, "Don't damage the book." You have told him what not to do but you have not told him what to do. So blocks have begun in that child and now they will become more entangled, and one day there will only be these blocks. There will only be 'don't do this, don't do that' inside him. He will not understand what he should do.

What I mean by a creative way is that he should be told what to do. If he is banging the glass it means that he has energy and he wants to do something. You have said don't do this; it would be better if you give him some clay and say, "Make a glass. Make a glass just like this glass."

This would be a creative use of his energy. Do you understand me? When he went to pick flowers you could have given him some paper and said, "Make a flower like this one." This would have been a creative use of his energy. He is tearing up a book or has picked up a book: you should give him something else to do so that he can use his energy.

Nowadays education is totally uncreative, which is why the life of a child is ruined right from the beginning. We are all ruined children – the only difference is that we are adults. Otherwise we are all ruined children: right from our childhood everything has gone wrong and then all our lives we go on doing these wrong things.

As I said, creativity means that whenever energy arises it should be used in a creative way so that something emerges out of it and nothing is destroyed. The energy that someone uses to always criticize everyone can be used to write a song. And do you know? – it is the people who cannot write a song and cannot write poetry who become critics. It is the same energy. Critics also have the same energy to write a song or to create a poem, but they don't use it in a creative way. All they do is criticize others: who is writing badly and who is doing what. This is a destructive use. The world could become a much better place if we were to use our energy, all the energy inside us, in a creative way.

And remember that energy is never good or bad. Even the energy of anger is not good or bad, it all depends on how it is used. Don't think that the energy of anger is bad; energy cannot be good or bad. Even atomic energy is neither good nor bad: with it the whole world can be destroyed and a whole world can be created. All energy is neutral, no energy is good or bad. If used for destructive purposes it becomes bad, if used creatively it becomes good.

So you should change the way you use the energy of anger, of desire, of sex, of hatred, and use it in a creative way. Just as when someone brings manure it smells very bad, it stinks, but the gardener uses it in his garden, waters it and sows seeds. Through these seeds the manure becomes a tree. And the stink of manure passes through the veins of the tree and converts into the fragrance of the flowers. This same dirt, this same manure which used to smell bad becomes a flower and gives out a sweet fragrance. This is a transformation of energy. This is a transmutation of energy.

Everything about you that gives off a bad smell can change into something sweet-smelling – the same things – because what stinks can also smell sweet. So don't feel guilty if there is anger inside you – this is energy and you are fortunate to have it. And don't think that you are too sexual – this is just energy and you are fortunate that it is there. It would be unfortunate if you had no sexuality, it would be unfortunate if you could not get angry, if you were impotent. Then you would be useless because there would be no energy in you which could be used. So you are fortunate to have this energy. Be grateful for all the energies inside you. Now it is up to you how you use it.

All the great men in the world have been very sexual. It would be strange if they had not been sexual, because if they had not been they could not have become great.

You know about Gandhi – he was very sexual. And the day his father died...the doctors had told him that his father would not survive, but even on that night he could not be near his father – when his father died he was making love with his wife. The doctors had already told him that his father would not survive the night and that he should be by his bedside during the night; it was certain that he would not survive the night. Gandhi was very repentant about this: "What kind of a man am I?" But he should have been grateful for his sexuality because that same sexuality made him a celibate – the same energy! If he had sat next to his father that night, it is certain that no Gandhis would have been born into this world. Under the same circumstances most of us would have stayed with our fathers not just one night, even two nights – but there would have been no Gandhis. What must have seemed like a bad smell to him on that night later on became the fragrance of his life.

So don't reject any energy. Don't reject any energy that arises in you. Consider it a blessing and try to transform it. All energy can be changed and can be transformed. And what appears to you to be bad can be transformed into something fragrant, something beautiful.

I have discussed some of the questions, so the remaining ones we will discuss tomorrow.

THE PATH OF MEDITATION

understanding the mind

Chapter 4

My Beloved Ones,

THIS MORNING I spoke about the first step for a seeker. I also spoke about the different ways to purify the body. In the second layer of man's personality are his thoughts. The body should be pure and the mind should also be pure. The third layer is the emotions, and when the emotions are pure then the foundation for meditation is ready. When these three things have happened you will experience great joy. There will be tremendous peace in your life. If these three things have been accomplished, you will have a new life.

But these are just the basic steps to prepare you for meditation. In a sense, they are the outer practice. The inner practice is still deeper – in it we surrender the body, thoughts and emotions to purify them and make them empty. In the outer practice the body is purified, in the inner practice the body is surrendered. You enter a bodiless state, you enter a state of no-mind and you enter a state which is free of emotions. But before this can happen it is first necessary to remove the impurities within yourself.

I have spoken to you about the body; now I will speak about thoughts. What are the impurities of the mind?

Thoughts are very whimsical. Thoughts also leave an impression on the mind, whether good or bad. The things that a person thinks will also affect his personality. If someone is thinking of beauty, if a person is constantly reflecting on beauty, it is quite natural that it will also make his personality more beautiful. If someone is thinking about God, about the divine, and his thoughts revolve around this, it is natural that his life will become filled with the divine. If someone is thinking about truth it is natural that truth will become part of him.

In this context I would like to ask you to reflect on the things which are constantly on your mind. What do you think about all the time? Most of you are either thinking about money, sex or power.

Many years ago there was a king in China. One day he went to the border of his kingdom which was by the ocean, and he took his chief minister with him. They were both standing at the top of a hill watching the ocean which stretched for miles. There were many ships sailing by, coming and going, and the king asked the minister, "How many ships are coming in and how many are going out?"

The minister replied, "My lord, if you want the truth, there are only three ships coming in and three going out."

The king said, "Three? There are so many ships out there, don't you see them?"

The minister replied, "I have seen only three ships: one of money, one of sex and one of power. We spend our whole lives traveling on these three ships."

This is true: our thought processes travel on these three ships. And anyone who travels on these ships will not become pure in thought. He will have pure thoughts only when he gets off these three ships. So it is important for everyone to observe the thoughts that recur in his mind; what are the wounds in his mind around which his thoughts revolve. The thoughts to which his mind returns again and again will be his basic weakness. So everyone must discover this: is it money, is it sex or is it power? Do you constantly think about one of these things? Do you think about lying? Do you think about dishonesty, about cheating? These are all the minor things, the first three are the major points. If your mind revolves around these three then your thoughts are impure. They are called impure thoughts because as long as you are thinking them you cannot know truth.

Purity of thought is the same as what in India we call truth, goodness and beauty. Pure thoughts focus on these three states. How much do you think about truth? Do you think about truth at all? Do you ever wonder what truth is? In a quiet moment, does your mind ever wonder about it? Are you ever in anguish over the thought of truth? Do you ever feel you want to understand what beauty is? Do you ever feel you want to understand what happiness is?

If your mind is troubled by impure thoughts, then your mind is impure, and it is not possible to attain to enlightenment with an impure mind.

Impure thoughts take you outwards and pure thoughts take you inside. Impure thoughts flow outwards and downwards and pure thoughts flow inwards and upwards. It is impossible for someone who is thinking of truth, of goodness, of beauty, to not find his life colored by them.

Gandhi was once in prison. He used to constantly think about truth, about renunciation, about non-attachment. In those days he used to eat ten dates soaked overnight in water for breakfast. Vallabhbhai Patel was also in jail with him. He wondered, "Is this any kind of breakfast, just ten dates? How can it be enough?"

He used to soak the dates for Gandhi, so one day he soaked fifteen dates. He thought, "How will this old man know whether there are ten dates or fifteen? He will just eat them."

Gandhi saw that there were a few more dates. He said, "Vallabhbhai, please count the dates."

When the dates were counted there were fifteen of them. Gandhi said, "There are fifteen."

Vallabhbhai said, "What difference will it make if there are ten or fifteen?"

Gandhi closed his eyes and thought for a few minutes. He said, "Vallabhbhai, you have given me a great idea. You said, 'What is the difference between ten and fifteen?' so I have understood that there is no difference between ten and five either."

Gandhi said, "From today onwards I will only eat five dates. You have shown me a most wonderful thing, that there is no difference between ten and fifteen.

Vallabhbhai became afraid. He said, "I said that only so that you would eat a little more. I never imagined that you would think this way."

Someone who is always thinking about eating less and less will always give this kind of answer, and someone who is thinking about eating more will not see any difference between ten and fifteen. But for someone who continuously thinks of eating less and less, there is no difference between five and ten. So what you think will begin to show in your daily habits.

I will tell you one more story....

Gandhi used to drink warm water with a little honey and lime in it. Mahadev Desai was his close companion, and one day he was preparing the warm water for him. The water was hot, boiling hot; there was steam coming out of it. When Gandhi came after a few minutes Mahadev Desai gave him the water. Gandhi looked at it for a moment and said, "It would have been better if you had covered it."

Mahadev said, "What can happen in five minutes? And I was watching it, nothing fell in it."

Gandhi said, "It is not a question of anything falling into it. There is steam coming out of it which must have hurt some organisms." Gandhi said, "It is not a question of covering it or anything falling into it, but there is steam coming out of it and it must have harmed many organisms in the air. There is no other reason, but they could have been saved."

It is natural for someone who is always thinking of non-violence to think and act like this. So I tell you, if you are continuously thinking about something it will bring about a change in your everyday behavior.

This morning a friend came with this news. He said, "It is very sad that in spite of inviting some people twice, they are still not here, they are ten minutes late." He felt sad that in spite of inviting people twice, they had not come. If it were me, I would say instead that it is nice that so many people have come after being invited only twice, and I would say that it would have been even nicer if the people who didn't come could also be here. This would be the non-violent approach. His was a violent approach, there was violence in it.

So what I am saying to you is that if you think a little, if you create a few devices for yourself to purify your thoughts, you will find that slowly, slowly there will be changes in even your smallest actions. Even your language will become non-violent, your movements will become non-violent. Your thoughts can transform your whole life. Whatever you think has an effect on your life because your thoughts have immense power.

So much depends on what you think about all the time. If you are constantly thinking of money and you are trying to meditate, then you are moving in two opposing directions. It is just as if you were to tie two buffalos, one on each end of a cart. The cart will break in two with the force of the buffalos pulling in opposite directions, and it will not move forward.

If your thoughts are pure then you will find that there will be immense changes in even your smallest acts. Life is not made of great deeds, it is made up of small things. How you get up, how you sit, how you talk, what you say – much depends on this. And the main source from where all this action emerges is the mind.

So your thoughts should be oriented towards truth, goodness and beauty. Let there be a constant remembrance of truth in your life. Whenever you find time, reflect on truth, reflect on goodness and on beauty. And whenever you are about to do something, before you begin, think for a moment whether what you are about to do will be in harmony with truth, goodness and beauty or against them. If there are thoughts in your mind, consider whether this flow of thoughts is conducive to truth, to goodness and to beauty. If it is the opposite, then stop these thoughts immediately, don't encourage them. They will be harmful to you, they will pull you down and ruin your life. So be aware of the kinds of thoughts that are running through your head and with courage, effort, perseverance and determination divert them towards purity and truth.

Many times you will feel that you don't even know what truth is. Many times you will think that you don't even know what goodness is. It is possible that you may not be able to decide, but at least you have thought about it and have tried to find out. This in itself is good and will bring about changes in you. And someone who is continuously reflecting will slowly, slowly realize that he knows what truth and what goodness is.

Before every thought, every word and every act, stop for a moment. There is no hurry. See what you are about to do, what its result will be. What does it tell you? What will happen as a result of it? It is very important for a seeker to think this way.

So the first thing about the basic purification of thought is to observe what the central focus of your thoughts is. If you don't focus in any one of the ways that I am talking about, then it will be helpful for you to develop this practice.

You will be surprised to know that of the three aspects – truth, goodness, beauty – if even one is active in you then the other two will also automatically become active. And I should mention to you that there are three types of people. One type has a possibility for a quick awakening of the truth aspect, the second type has a possibility for a quick blossoming of the aspect of goodness and the third type has a possibility for a quick blossoming of the aspect of beauty.

For each of you there will be one dominant aspect, but if even one aspect becomes active then the other two will automatically become active. If a person is a lover of beauty he will not be a liar because lying is such an ugly thing. If a person is a lover of beauty he will not be able to do any wrong because it is so ugly to do any wrong. This means that he will not be able to steal because stealing is so ugly. So if he is totally devoted to beauty, much can become possible because of it.

Once, Gandhi was a guest at Rabindranath Tagore's house. Rabindranath was old at the time. He was a lover of beauty; he was not concerned with truth or goodness. This only means that these were not his direct paths – he was a lover of beauty. Gandhi was his guest. It was evening and the two were about to go out for a walk when Rabindranath said, "Wait a moment, I would like to comb my hair."

Gandhi said, "What an absurd thing to say! Comb your hair?"

Gandhi had shaved his head so he did not have the problem of combing his hair. And in his old age to worry about combing one's hair was a bit strange, and for Gandhi it was unthinkable. He waited a bit angrily but he could not say anything to Rabindranath.

Rabindranath went inside. Two minutes passed, five minutes passed, ten minutes passed. Gandhi was surprised that he was taking so long. What was he doing inside? He looked through the window and saw that Rabindranath was standing before a full-length mirror, combing his hair. Gandhi simply could not tolerate this anymore. He said, "I cannot understand what you are doing! The time for our walk is being wasted. And why do you need to comb your hair? What is the point of combing your hair at your age?"

Rabindranath went outside and he said, "When I was young it would not have mattered if I did not comb my hair, but now that I have become old it will not do if I don't comb it. And don't think that I am trying to look good; I just don't want to disturb anyone by appearing ugly to them." Rabindranath said, "Don't think that I'm doing this to look good. The body which I am beautifying and moving around in will turn into ashes tomorrow. I know that one day soon it will be on a burning pyre and will turn to ashes. But I don't want to be an ugly sight; I don't want to disturb anyone – this is why I give it all this attention."

A lover of beauty like Rabindranath will think in these terms. Ugliness is a type of violence towards others. This ugliness can be in any form: it can be in your behavior, in your language or in any other form.

So if you would like to appear to be beautiful, then do it with totality. Become completely beautiful so that your whole life becomes beautiful.

So I don't say that the person who is combing his hair is doing something wrong. I am only saying that besides your hair, there is something else that needs to be beautified. I am not saying that if you are wearing jewelry you are doing something wrong; I am saying that it is okay if you are wearing jewelry, but why not also *be* a jewel? You have come here wearing spotlessly white clothes. It is good that you are wearing white clothes, but make your inner self also as white as that.

So try to understand what beauty is and you will find that truth and goodness will automatically follow. If you try to understand what goodness is you will also understand beauty and truth. If you try to understand truth you will get the other two also. You can make any of these three your foundation. If one of these is of any interest to you, make it your focus and let all your thoughts revolve around it. Allow your interiority to be touched by it. Choose one of these three and concentrate on it. And if you practice it throughout your life, in every aspect of your life – in your behavior and in your actions – slowly, slowly you will observe a strange phenomenon happening: you will be amazed to find that the more you practice it, the more all the unnatural things in your life and all the impure thoughts will become weaker.

I am not asking you to stop thinking about money. What I am saying is that you should start thinking more of goodness, beauty and truth. When you start thinking of beauty you will not be able to think about money, because there is nothing so ugly as thinking about money. When you think about beauty you will not be able to think about sex because there is no uglier state of mind than to be thinking about sex. So I am emphatically telling you to direct your energy to those states, and you will find that slowly, slowly your energy will return from the useless thoughts and the grip that they have over you will disappear.

With great awareness drop all that is impure and with awareness concentrate on that which is pure. When your thoughts become pure there will be tremendous changes in your life. This is the most important thing about thoughts. It is very important if you want to purify your thoughts.

Then there are some minor things which I would also like to say. It is important for you to know that all of your thoughts come from the outside. None of them come from within, they all come from the outside. There may be some inner basis for the thought inside you, but remember that all your thoughts come from the outside. The thoughts themselves come from the outside but there are grooves along which they run inside you .

If someone thinks about money, the thought of money must have come from the outside but the desire for money comes from inside, its seed is inside. The thoughts come from the outside and then attach themselves to your desires. If someone is thinking of sex the desire for sex comes from outside, but there is a seed inside to which this desire attaches itself. Your thought comes from outside but there is a seed for this thought inside you. All your thoughts come from the outside.

To purify your thoughts it is important to realize that the thoughts which enter your mind don't come accidentally. You should be alert to the fact that the thoughts which enter you are the ones that you actually want; the rest you just throw away.

As I said earlier, if someone is throwing garbage into your house you will fight with that person, but if someone is throwing garbage into your mind you will not fight with him. If I meet you on the road and start telling you the story of a movie, you will not object. But if I come to your house and throw some garbage into your house you will ask me, "What are you doing? This is not right!" And if I fill your mind with garbage, if I tell you the story of a movie you will listen to it very happily.

You are not aware that your mind can also be filled with garbage. You are each others' enemies: you keep on dumping garbage into each others' minds. What are the people that you consider to be your friends doing to you? – nobody betrays you more than they do. Your enemies are better than they are; at least your enemies don't fill your head with rubbish because they don't talk to you.

You are all filling each others' heads with garbage and you are so fast asleep that you don't realize what you are taking in. You take everything in. You are like a guesthouse where there are no caretakers and no guards outside to see who is coming in and who is going out. You are a place where anyone can come in man, animal, thief or cheat. And when he feels like it he can leave and if he doesn't feel like leaving he will stay.

Your mind should not be like a guesthouse. If your mind is like a guesthouse, if it is not well protected, then it will be difficult for you to become free of impure thoughts. You should consciously watch over your mind.

The second step towards achieving purity of thought is the need to watch your thoughts. There should be a certain watchfulness. You should be constantly watching what is happening inside you and rejecting whatsoever is useless.

Recently, I was traveling. There were two of us in the train compartment, another man and myself. He wanted to chat with me. As soon as I sat down in my seat he offered me a cigarette. I said, "I am sorry, but I don't smoke."

He put the cigarette back. A little while later he took out a betel leaf and offered it to me: "Please accept it."

I said, "I am sorry, but I don't want it."

Again he put it away and sat down. Then he picked up his newspaper and asked me, "Would you like to read it?"

I said, "I don't want to read."

Then he said to me, "It is so difficult – you refuse to accept whatever I offer you."

I said, "A person who simply accepts everything is a fool. And with what you are offering me I would also try to keep away from you. I will not take it, but I also wish it were taken away from you."

If you have nothing to do, what do you do? You will pick up the newspaper and start reading it because you have nothing to do. It would be better to simply sit and do nothing than to collect all that junk. There is nothing wrong with doing nothing, but there are some fools who say that it is better to do anything rather than to do nothing. This is not true. It is always better to do nothing than to do something harmful, because at least in those moments you are not losing anything and you are not collecting any rubbish.

So be aware about this. If you watch the movement of thoughts inside you it is not difficult to keep your thoughts pure. And it is not difficult to recognize impure thoughts: thoughts that create a kind of restlessness inside you are impure thoughts and thoughts that create a flow of peace inside you are pure thoughts. Thoughts that bring joy to you are pure and thoughts that create any kind of disturbance are impure thoughts. You have to avoid such thoughts. And if you constantly watch your mind, your ·

thoughts will become more and more pure.

And the third thing: there are many impure thoughts in the world that keep on repeating. These impure thoughts create a fire, and the smoke from these impure thoughts enters into your consciousness and surrounds you and smothers you. But don't forget that there are a few flames of pure thought still burning, there are still a few waves of pure thought alive. In this whole ocean of darkness there are still a few sources of light. Try to be close to these. This is what I call *satsang*.

Although the world is very dark it is not all darkness, there are a few lamps burning. Even if they are made of clay and even if the wick is small, at least they exist. You should try to be close to them because when you take your unlit lamp to one which is lit, there is every possibility that by being so close to a lighted lamp the unlit lamp will light up again. It is possible that it too will lose the smoke and start burning bright again.

Move closer to the flames that stand for truth, goodness and beauty. Bring yourself closer to them. Move closer to those thoughts, to those people, into the waves of those thoughts where it becomes possible to light your lamp.

You can do this in three ways: by being close to pure and true thoughts, by being close to pure and true people, and mainly and most importantly, by being close to nature. Nature never has impure thoughts. If you look at the sky and you go on looking at it, you will find that the sky does not encourage any impure thoughts in you. Instead it will clear all the rubbish in your head and you will find that by looking at the sky you feel you have become one with it. If you look at a waterfall you will feel that you have become part of the waterfall. If you are in a forest full of greenery you will feel you have also become one of the trees.

Once a man asked a sage, "I would like to know truth. How do I do it?"

The sage said, "There are too many people at the moment, come back when there is no one around."

He did not go to see the sage the whole day, he waited until the evening when there was no one around. It was dark, the lamps were being lit and the sage was alone. He was just about to close his door when the man said, "Wait! Now there is no one. You have seen all the people who came to see you. I have been waiting outside for everyone to leave so that I could come in. Now I am here and I want to ask you how I can become silent and how I can get enlightened?"

The sage replied, "Come outside. It is not possible in this hut because the lamp which is burning has been made by man. And it is not possible inside this hut because the hut itself has been made by man. Come outside. There is a big world outside which has not been created by any man, it was created by God. Come outside where there is no sign of human creation."

Remember, man is the only animal that leaves impure impressions behind; no other animal does that.

They went outside. There were bamboos, it was a full moon night and the moon was right overhead. The sage stood in front of the trees...one minute, two minutes, ten minutes, fifteen minutes...until the man asked, "Say something. You are just standing quietly. I don't understand."

The sage said, "If you could you would have understood. Simply stand quietly. I have become a bamboo and you can also become one."

The man said, "This is very difficult."

And the sage said, "This is my method. When I stand near these bamboos, after some time I forget that I am different and I become a bamboo. Looking at the moon, after some time I forget that I am different and I become the moon."

Being close to nature, if you can discover the oneness between yourself and nature, then in a mysterious way your thoughts will become pure. The impurity of your thoughts will begin to grow less. So there are three ways: purity of thought...and there are innumerable paths to the purity of thought. Pure beings never die out, they are forever present – but sometimes we are so blind that no living person ever seems pure to us. Only the dead people seem pure to us. But it is very difficult to commune with dead people, and yet all the religions of the world worship the dead. There is not a single religion that worships the living; they all worship dead people. And they have this false idea that all the great people who were to be born have already lived, and there cannot be more. And they have this idea that if a person is alive he cannot be divine.

There are always enlightened people on the Earth, they are present everywhere. If you have the eyes you can recognize them. And the important thing is that even if according to your judgments and expectations they are not absolutely pure, how does their impure past concern you?

There was a fakir who used to say, "I have learned something from whoever I have met up to now. "

Someone asked him, "How is this possible? What can you learn from a thief?"

He said, "It happened once that for a month I was a guest at a thief's house. He would leave the house every night to go out and steal, and he would return at three or four o'clock in the morning. I would ask him, 'So, did anything happen?'

He would reply, "Nothing today, maybe tomorrow."

He did not manage to steal anything for the whole month. Sometimes there was a guard at the door, sometimes the people of the house would wake up, sometimes he could not break the lock, sometimes he entered a house but could not manage to steal anything. And every night the thief would return home tired and I would ask him, "So, did anything happen?" And he would say, "Not today, but maybe I will manage tomorrow."

"This is what I learned from him: if it does not happen today, don't worry. Remember, it might happen tomorrow. When a thief who has gone out to steal, to do something wrong, can be so full of hope…."

So the fakir said, "In the days when I was searching for God, I wanted to *steal* God. I was feeling the walls and knocking on doors but I could not find the way. I was tired and disheartened and I thought, 'It is hopeless. Just drop it.' But that thief saved me – just by saying, 'It did not happen today, but maybe it will happen tomorrow.' And I have made this into a maxim: if not today, maybe tomorrow. And then one day it happened – the thief managed to steal something and I also found the divine."

So it is not that you can learn only from a realized man. You have to have the intelligence and understanding to learn, and then for you the whole world is full of realized people. If they are not available, then....

For instance, there were people who passed by Mahavira and thought that he was just a scoundrel, a naked man: "Who knows who this man is? Maybe he is a madman!" There were many people who did not recognize Mahavira. You may have heard people say that a man is a *nangaluchcha*: this word was first used to describe Mahavira because he was naked, *nanga*, and he used to shave his head, *luchcha*. People used to say, "He's a nangaluchcha." Nowadays this word is considered to be an insult. In India, if someone calls you this you will get angry. But it was first used for that naked and shaved sage, Mahavira. So there were people who passed by Mahavira and thought, "Who knows what kind of person he must be?" There were people who hit him and beat him. They thought that he was a fraud, a scoundrel, some kind of infiltrator. These were people who did not understand Mahavira.

There were people who crucified Christ thinking that he was a liar. There were people who poisoned Socrates. And don't think that such people were only around in those days; they are present inside each of you. This is how people are. Even now, if you had the opportunity you would poison Socrates, and given half a chance you would crucify Christ again. And if you had the opportunity you would look at

Mahavira and laugh at this madman.

But since they are dead and you revere the dead, they are not a problem. It is difficult to revere someone who is alive. It is difficult to accept him and to understand him. So if you are really seeking for truth then the whole world is full of enlightened people. It has never happened and it will never happen that there are no enlightened people available. And the day it happens that the chain of enlightened people stops, from that day on no one will become enlightened any-more because the very stream itself will have come to an end. It will have become a desert. Wide or narrow, the stream has always been flowing. Be familiar with it, be con-nected with it. It is not that when you find an enlightened person you will immediately understand. But if you keep your eyes open, understanding will come through small things.

In one book, I was reading about a sage who was still working at the age of sixty. His name was Rajababu, as his mother had called him. He had become old but people still called him Rajababu. One day he went out for a stroll. The sun had not yet risen and he walked to the outskirts of the village. A woman was trying to wake up her son saying to him, "Rajababu, how long are you going to keep on sleeping? It is morning now, wake up."

He was walking with a stick in his hand when he heard, "Rajababu, how long are you going to keep on sleeping? It is morning now. Wake up."

He heard this, turned around and went back home. He felt, "Now it will be difficult… today I have received my message. Today I heard, 'Rajababu, how long are you going to keep on sleeping? It is already morning, now wake up!'" And he said, "Enough is enough! Now it is finished."

Now who knows which woman was saying this to wake up her child – but for someone with understanding it becomes a divine message. And it is possible that someone is trying to teach you something and you don't have the ears to hear or the eyes to see. You are just sitting and listening, thinking that maybe it is meant for someone else.

So be close to truth, long for truth, search for truth, discover and nourish pure thoughts in your life, be close to nature These are all helpful conditions and foundations for the development of pure thoughts.

Now I have given you a few indications for the purification of thoughts, but you will have to understand their importance to make them part of your daily practice. It is not only for today or tomorrow: there cannot be a meditation camp where in three days the thing happens and the matter is finished. Irreligiousness is a disease that pervades life, so the meditation camp will also have to go on for your whole life. There is no way out, it will have to be practiced throughout your whole life.

Tomorrow I will talk about how to purify the emotions.

Now we will try to understand something about the evening meditation and then we will sit for the meditation.

For the evening meditation we will make a resolution like we have done for the morning meditation. We will repeat the resolution five times. Then after these five times, for a while we will feel it, the same as we have done this morning. Everyone should be lying down...everyone should lie down beforehand. Lie down quietly in your place and then the lights will be switched off. Then we will relax our bodies. In the last meditation camp I asked you to relax your whole body. It is possible that some of you were not able to do it, but I have a suggestion for them.

In yoga there are seven centers or *chakras*. Out of these seven we will use five for this meditation. The first chakra is called the *muladhar* and it is near the sex center. It is the first chakra that we will use in this nightly meditation. The second chakra is called the *svadhishthan*. Assume that it is near the navel. For now you can just imagine this, that the first chakra is near the sex center and the second one close to the navel. Next, the chakra near the heart is called the *anahat* chakra. The chakra on the forehead is called *agya*, and if you move further up the chakra at the top of the head is called the *sahasrar* chakra. We will use these five. There are more chakras — there are seven chakras — but we will use only these five and with their help we will get our bodies to relax.

You will be surprised to know that the first chakra controls the legs. We will give suggestions to the first chakra. When you lie down I will ask you to focus on the first chakra, so then you will place your attention near the sex center and keep your focus there. Then I will say: let the first chakra relax. And with that, both legs should relax. You should imagine that the first chakra is relaxing, that it is relaxing, and the legs are relaxing. In a little while you will find that your legs have become lifeless and are just hanging from your body.

When the legs have relaxed then we will move upwards

to the second chakra near the navel. I will ask you to bring your awareness to the navel; you will focus your attention on the navel. Then I will say that the second chakra is becoming relaxed, all the organs in the abdomen are becoming relaxed. With this suggestion all the organs *will* become relaxed.

Then we will move further, to the heart center, and I will say that the heart chakra is relaxing. Then you will relax your heart. Your awareness should be on the heart chakra, near the heart, and you will feel that the heart chakra is becoming relaxed. Then the whole area, the whole mechanism of the chest will relax.

Then we will move upwards: on the forehead, between the two eyes is the agya chakra, the third-eye center. We will direct our awareness to the third eye, and I will say that the third-eye center is becoming relaxed and the forehead is re-laxed. And with that the forehead, the neck and the whole area of the head will become totally relaxed, and the whole body will relax There will be a slight heaviness and only at the top of the head will there be a little vibration.

And finally I will direct you to the sahasrar chakra, the seventh center, and you will bring your awareness to the top of your head. This too will relax and with it the whole head will relax. Through these suggestions you will find that everything inside you has become relaxed. I have created this long process so that everyone's body becomes as relaxed as a dead body.

I will give suggestions to these five chakras, and when all of them have become relaxed I will say that the body has be-come totally dead, now drop it completely. When the body has become lifeless, then I will say that your breathing is re-laxing, is becoming quieter. I will suggest this for a while.

Then I will suggest that the mind is becoming totally empty. So I will be giving three suggestions: one for the chakras, then one for the breath, and the third for the thoughts.

After this whole exercise I will say that for ten minutes everything will be silent. In that silence you will only experience the witness inside you. There will be a light of awareness and you will be quietly lying there. Only your awareness will be there, there will only be an awareness of lying there. In this stage it is possible that the whole body will feel as if it is dead – and it will, because through the exercise with the chakras the body will become like a dead body.

Don't be afraid. Don't be afraid if the body feels as if it is dead. It is good to feel like this. If a person experiences his body as being dead while he is alive, he will slowly become free of his fears about death. So don't be afraid. Whatever experiences you go through – light, brightness, peace – just observe it and be where you are in total emptiness. These three stages are very important: the determination, the feeling and the meditation. This will be the nightly meditation.

I think you have all understood what I have said. Now you can all spread out. First find a place for yourself so that you can lie down. Nobody should be sitting. Give yourself as much space as possible, make use of the whole space.

THE PATH OF MEDITATION

understanding emotions

Chapter 5

My Beloved Ones,

WE HAVE TALKED about two phases that are related to the spiritual journey: purity of the body and purity of thought. Emotions are at a deeper level than the body and thoughts. The purity of emotions is the most important quality. On the spiritual journey and in meditation, the purity of emotions is more useful than that of the body and of thoughts. This is so because man does not live so much according to thoughts, he lives more according to his emotions. It is said that man is a rational animal, but this is not true. You don't do very many things in your life as a result of thinking, most of what you do is influenced by your emotions. Your hatred, your anger, your love – all these are related to your emotions, not to your thoughts.

Most of the activities in life originate from the world of emotions, not from the world of thoughts. You must also have noticed that you think one thing, and when the time comes you do something else. The reason for this is that there is a fundamental difference between emotions and thinking. You may decide that you will not become angry; you may think that anger is bad but when anger gets hold of you thinking is left aside and you become angry.

As long as a transformation in the world of emotions does not happen, just thinking and contemplation alone cannot bring about a revolution in life. That's why on the spiritual

118

journey the most basic point is the emotions. So this morning we will discuss how to bring about the purification of the emotions.

Of the many dimensions that emotions cover I would like to emphasize four. I will talk about the four aspects through which emotions can become pure. These are also the four aspects that can reverse and become a womb for impure feelings. The first of these aspects is friendliness, the second is compassion, the third is cheerfulness and the fourth is gratitude. If you were to include these four emotions in your life you would achieve purity of emotions.

These four each have their opposite. The opposite of friendliness is hatred and enmity, the opposite of compassion is cruelty, violence and unkindness, the opposite of cheerfulness is sadness, misery, anguish and worry, the opposite of gratitude is ingratitude. Someone whose life and emotions are in the four opposite aspects is in a state of impure emotions, and someone who is rooted in the first four aspects is rooted in pure emotions.

You should find out what influences your emotions, what moves your emotions. Is it true that instead of friendliness, enmity and hostility are more prominent in your life? Is it true that instead of friendliness you are more easily moved by enmity, by hostility? Are you more easily impressed by it? Are you more easily triggered by it? Do you get more energy from it? As I said earlier anger has energy, but friendliness also has energy. Someone who only knows how to generate the energy of anger will miss a major dimension in his life. Someone who has not learned how to awaken the energy of friendliness is someone who is powerful only in hostile situations and becomes weak in friendly situations.

You might not be aware that all the nations in the world become weaker during times of peace, and during times of war they become more powerful. Why? – because they don't know how to create the energy of friendliness. Silence is not a strength for you, it is a weakness. This is the reason why India, a nation that has talked so much about peace and love, became so powerless – because ordinarily the only way to feel strength is to be hostile.

Hitler wrote in his autobiography: If you want to make a nation powerful then pretend that you have enemies or create real enemies. Tell the nation that there are enemies everywhere, even if there are not. When people believe that they are surrounded by enemies it will generate much strength and energy.

This is why Hitler pretended that the Jews were the enemy – it was not true – and for ten years he preached and explained to the whole country that, "The Jews are our enemies and we will have to protect ourselves from them." Much energy was generated. All of Germany's strength came out of hostility, all of Japan's strength came out of hostility. Today, the power of America and Russia also comes out of hostility.

Up to now the history of mankind shows that we only know how to generate the energy of enmity; we don't know about the energy of friendliness. Mahavira, Buddha and Christ laid the foundations for the energy of friendliness. They have said that non-violence is power. Christ said "Love is power"; Buddha said "Compassion is power." You hear it, but you don't understand.

So I say to you, think about your life. When do you feel powerful? – is it when you feel animosity towards someone or is it when you are feeling peaceful and full of love towards someone? And you will see that you feel powerful in hostile conditions; and when you are in a state of awareness and silence you become powerless and weak. This means that you are being ruled by impure emotion. And the stronger the impure emotions are, the less you can enter within yourself.

What is it that prevents you from entering within yourself? Try to understand this very important point. Your hostility is always focused on the outside; this means that hostility happens towards someone who is outside of you. If there were no one on the outside hostility could not arise in you.

But I tell you that love is not focused on the outside: even if there is no one on the outside love can still happen within you. Love is intrinsic, friendliness is intrinsic. Hostility needs the other, it is related to the other. Hatred is triggered by the outside, love wells up inside. The spring of love flows from within, the reaction of hatred is provoked from without. Impure emotions are created on the outside, pure emotions flow from within.

Try to understand this difference between impure emotions and pure emotions. The emotions that are triggered by the outside are not pure; so your love, the passion that you call love, is not pure because it is triggered by the outside. Only the love that flows from within, that is not triggered by the outside, is pure. That's why in the East we say there is a difference between love and passion: we separate passion from love.

Passion is triggered by the outside. Buddha or Mahavira have no passion in their hearts, they have love.

Jesus was passing through a town. It was noon and he was very tired. The sun was very hot so he stopped to rest in a garden under a tree. The house and garden belonged to a prostitute. She saw Jesus resting under the tree in her garden. No one like this had ever stopped to rest in her garden; she had never seen anyone like this before. She had seen many beautiful people, she had seen many powerful people, but this beauty was different, this wholeness was something not of this world. She was so pulled by her attraction to him that before she realized it she had already reached the tree.

When she went close to Jesus and began to look at him, his eyes opened and he got up to leave. He thanked her saying, "Thank you for the shade that your tree has given me. Now I'm going, I have a long way to go."

But the prostitute said, "If you don't come inside my house for a little while, I will feel offended. Please stay for a while. This is the first time that I am inviting someone into my house. People come to my door and I send them away. This is the first time in my life that I am inviting someone in."

Jesus said, "Once you have invited me into your heart, I have already become your guest. But I have a long way to go so please allow me to leave. I have already received your hospitality."

But the prostitute said, "This hurts me. Won't you even show enough love to enter my house?"

Jesus told her, "Remember, I'm the only person who *can* love you. All the other men who come to your door don't love you. I am the only person who can love you. The others who come to your door don't love you because they don't have love. They have come because of you. With me, my love is within me."

Love is like the light of a lamp: if no one were here the light would still continue to fall on emptiness, and if someone were to pass it would fall on them. But passion and desire are not like light: when they are triggered by someone, these energies move towards them. That's why passion is a tension. Love is not a tension. There is no tension in love, love is a state of absolute calmness.

Impure emotions are those which are influenced by the outside. The winds from the outside give rise to impure emotions within you. And pure emotions are those which come from within you; the winds from outside don't influence them. We don't think of Mahavira or Buddha in this way, that they loved – but I tell you that they were the only people who loved. But there is a difference between their love and yours. Your love is in relation to someone; their love is not a relationship, it is a state of being. It is not a relationship – their love is not in relation to someone else, it is their state of being. They are compelled to love because they have no other choice.

It is said about Mahavira that people insulted him, they threw stones at him, they put nails into his ear and he forgave everything. I say that this is not true: Mahavira didn't forgive anyone because only people who get angry can forgive. And Mahavira did not have pity on them because only those who are cruel can have pity. And Mahavira didn't think that he shouldn't behave badly with these people because only people who behave badly think like that.

So what did Mahavira do? Mahavira was helpless, he had nothing to give except love. No matter what was done to him his only answer would be love. If you throw a stone at a tree full of fruit you will get only fruit as an answer, there is no other way. The tree is not doing anything, this is its helplessness. And if you drop any kind of bucket into a river full of water, whether the bucket is dirty or clean, made of gold or iron, the river has no choice but to give you water. There is nothing great about the river, it is helpless to do otherwise. So when love is a state of being it is a kind of choicelessness – one has to give, there is no other way.

So the emotions which come from within, which don't pull you from outside, which cannot be pulled from the outside, are pure emotions. And the waves of emotion that the storms outside create within you are impure emotions. Emotions created by the outside will cause restlessness and worry inside you, and the ones that arise from within you will fill you with bliss.

So remember this first thing about pure and impure emotion: pure emotion is a state of being, impure emotion is a distortion of being, not a state. Impure emotion is the result of outside influence on being, pure emotion is an inner expansion of being. So think about this: do the emotions that move you come from within you, or do other people create them in you?

I am walking on the street and you insult me: if I get angry this is impure emotion because you have created it in me. I am walking on the street: you show me respect and I am pleased – this is impure emotion because you have created it in me. But if my inner state remains the same as it was before the insult or the praise, whether you swear at me or you praise me, this is pure emotion because you did not create it in me, it is my own. That which is my own is pure. That which is my own is pure and that which comes from the outside is impure. What comes from the outside is a reaction, an echo.

Recently I went to a place where you can hear echoes. If you make a sound there the mountains repeat it. I have said that most people only echo: if you say anything they will repeat it. They don't have anything of their own to say, they are like echo chambers. If you scream they scream back – it is not theirs, you have created it. And what you gave was not yours, someone else created it in you. You are all echo chambers: you don't have any sound of your own, any life of your own. You don't have any feeling of your own. All your emotions are impure because they belong to others, they are borrowed.

So remember this first key: emotion should be your own. It should not be a reaction, it should be the state of your being.

I have divided this state of being into four parts. The first is friendliness. Friendliness is a quality that has to be developed. Friendliness has to be developed because there is a source of friendliness within you, but life gives very few opportunities for it to develop. It remains undeveloped, it remains like a seed in the soil of your being – it cannot grow.

The seed of enmity is very developed. Why? There are natural reasons for this...because it also is needed. It may be needed, but it is not meant to be a lifelong companion. There are times when it is needed and there is also a time when letting go of it is needed.

When a child is born his first experience is not an experience of love. What a child experiences when he is born is fear. This is natural. The small child was very comfortable in his mother's womb where he had no problems, no worries about earning his living, eating – no worries. He was resting in a very blissful sleep. When he comes out of the mother's womb the small child, weak in every way, his first experience

125

is of fear. And if he gets a shock of fear he will not feel love towards the first person he sees, he will be afraid of that person. And if he is afraid of someone he will start to hate them.

Take this as a basic principle: fear never creates love. If someone says that there can be no love without fear, their statement is completely wrong. If there is fear, there is no possibility of love. There can never be love with fear. Even if love is shown superficially there is no love inside.

Most of the love that we see in this world is based on fear. And a love that is based on fear is false. That's why on the surface there is love but hatred keeps slipping out from inside. You also hate the person you love. Love is on the surface and hatred is below because you are afraid of people. Remember this: a person who intimidates others is missing the opportunity to receive love. If the father is intimidating his son he will not be able to get his love. If a husband is intimidating his wife he will not be able to get her love. He will get a pretense of love but he won't get love because love grows only in fearlessness, it doesn't grow in fear.

As soon as a child is born he experiences fear – and that's where the source of hatred is activated. The energy source of love is not activated. Most people die without this source ever becoming activated because life doesn't give it a chance. You think you love someone: that is also not love, it is only lust. Even that is only lust, even that is not love. Love can grow only through meditation.

This is why the source of love and friendliness within you has to be developed. It has to be developed in spite of all the primitive instincts which don't give it a chance to develop. The life that you lead doesn't allow it to grow, only hatred is developed. And what you call friendliness is only hypocrisy and politeness. Your friendliness is only an arrangement to escape from hatred, to avoid it – but it is not friendliness.

Friendliness is a completely different thing. How can you develop that source? How can feelings of friendliness begin to happen within you? You have to constantly create a milieu of friendliness around yourself. A message of friendliness has to be conveyed to all the people who are around you. Waves of friendliness have to be sent. And inside yourself you have to give it energy, you have to activate that space of friendliness.

When you are sitting on the bank of a river, give love to the river. I am talking about the river because to give love to a person could be a little difficult. Give love to a tree – I am talking about a tree because it may be hard to give love to a person. First of all, send love to nature. The anahat chakra, the heart center can flow more easily towards nature because nature is not wounding you.

In the ancient days people were amazing: they would send messages of love to the whole world! When the sun rose in the morning they would greet it with folded hands saying, "Glory to you! In your infinite compassion you give us light and radiance." And this worship was not pagan, it was not out of ignorance; it had meaning, it had great meaning. It would be impossible for someone who was filled with love for the sun, who just by calling the river his mother becomes filled with love, who calls the earth his mother and by remembering this is filled with love, to harbor a dislike for people for very long. It is not possible.

These were amazing people who gave messages of love to all of nature. They cultivated prayer, love and devotion everywhere. This is needed. If you want the seed of love inside you to sprout, the very first thing is to send a message of love to nature. But you are such strange people: the moon will be in the sky the whole night and you will be sitting and playing cards, and you will be calculating how much you have won or lost. The moon will be up there and a beautiful opportunity for love will be lost for nothing. The moon could have awakened that center of love within you. If you could sit with the moon for a few enchanted moments and convey a message of love, its rays could move something inside you, some essence, and you would be filled with love.

There are opportunities everywhere...there are opportunities *everywhere*. Existence is full of amazing things – give love to them. Whenever you get any opportunity to love, don't let it pass, use it. For example, you are walking along the road and there is a stone on the road – move it aside. This is an opportunity that comes completely free of charge, and it will transform your whole life. This work is very inexpensive! What could be a more inexpensive meditation than this? – you are walking on the road and you see a stone; you pick it up and put it on the side of the road. Who knows who might be passing by, and who knows who might be injured by the stone? You have carried out an act of love. I am telling you this because very small things in life cultivate the seed of love within you, very small, small things.

A child is crying on the street and you just pass by – can't you wait a few seconds and wipe the tears from his eyes?

Abraham Lincoln was in a Senate meeting when a pig got stuck in a gutter. He ran out of the meeting saying, "Hold the discussion for a minute, I'll be right back."

This was a very strange thing to do. The American parliament had probably never been stopped for such a thing. He ran out to free the pig! His clothes were all covered in mud. He took the pig out of the gutter and then went back inside. The people asked, "What was it? Why did you stop the meeting and run out so agitated?"

He answered, "A life was in danger."

This was such a simple act of love, but so amazing! And these small, small things.... And I see people who filter their water before drinking it so that no organism is killed, but there is no love inside them. Filtering the water has no value; it is a very mechanical habit to filter the water before drinking it. And they don't eat at night for fear that some organism will be killed, but there is no love in their hearts so this is just meaningless. It doesn't matter that they filter the water before drinking it or that they don't eat at night or that they don't eat meat – none of this matters. A *brahmin* or a Jaina will not eat meat, but don't think that it is because he is full of love inside – it is just a matter of habit. It is his conditioning, but he has no love inside him. Yes, if this develops through your love it will be an extraordinary thing.

Non-violence is the ultimate religion only when it has evolved through love. If it has been reached by reading scriptures or by following some tradition, then it is not religion. In life there are many small, small things, very small things. And you have forgotten....

What I am saying to you is that if you put your hand on someone's shoulder, then send him all the love in your heart through your hand. Let all your life-energy, your whole heart gather in your hand and then let it all go out. You will be surprised, magic will happen. When you look into someone's eyes, pour your whole heart through your eyes and you will be surprised: your eyes will become magical and they will move something inside the other person. Not only will your love awaken, but it may happen that you become the medium, the cause for someone else's love to awaken. When a man loves rightly, love becomes active inside thousands of people.

Don't miss any opportunity to awaken this center for friendliness and love. And to grasp this opportunity, remember this key: every day, during the course of these twenty-four hours, remember to do one or two things for which you expect nothing in return. You work for twenty-four hours a day and you do that because you want something in return. Regularly, every day, do something for which you don't expect to get anything in return. These will be acts of love and they will help to give birth to love inside you. If a person just does one thing every day for which he expects to get nothing back, he will get much out of it because this will activate and develop the love-center inside him.

So do something for which you don't want anything in return, nothing at all. That way, friendliness will slowly, slowly grow. A moment will come when you will be able to be friendly with someone who is a stranger. Then there will be more growth, and a moment will come when you will even be able to be friendly with someone who is your enemy. And then a moment will come when you will not discriminate between who is a friend and who is an enemy.

Mahavira has said, "Everyone is my friend. I feel no enmity towards anyone."

This is not a thought, it is a feeling. It is not a thought in the mind but a state in which you feel that no one is your enemy. And when does that 'no one is my enemy' state arise? It arises when *you* are no longer anyone's enemy. It is possible that Mahavira still had some enemies, but Mahavira is saying that no one is *his* enemy. What does this mean? It means that *he* was carrying no enmity. Mahavira is saying that he harbors no enmity. What a joyous moment that must be!

When you love a person so much joy arises: then can there be a limit to the joy someone experiences who is able to love the whole world? This does not cost anything, you lose nothing and you gain much. That's why I don't say that Mahavira and Buddha are renunciates: in this world they are the ones who have enjoyed life more than anyone. In this world they have enjoyed the most. You may be renunciates, but not them. They have opened so many doors of unlimited, infinite bliss. They have drunk and known the most supreme, the most beautiful, the divine in this world. And what do *you* know? – you don't know anything except poison. They have experienced the elixir.

You have to discipline your life for the ultimate moment when you will be able to extend your love to the whole world and rays of love will radiate from your heart. But for that to happen it will need a discipline. Make sure that you do a small act of love every day. Do it consciously. The whole day gives thousands of opportunities for you to express your love. But you have many bad habits: you miss all opportunities to express your love but you don't miss a single opportunity to express your hatred. The more opportunities you miss to express your hatred the better, and the more opportunities you can take to express your love the better. Let the

131

opportunities to hate pass by. Once in a while, let them pass by unused. And once in a while use the opportunities to love consciously. This will speed up the process of your meditation tremendously.

So the first key was friendliness, and the second key is compassion. Compassion is also a form of friendliness, but I am mentioning it separately because it also contains some other elements. What I mean by 'other elements' is that if you look at other people around you, you will feel compassion for them. Right now many people are sitting here: one never knows, by the evening one of them may have died. On some evening everyone will be dead anyway, one day we will all be gone. And if I realize that among all the people who are sitting in front of me I may not ever see one of their faces again, will my heart not fill with compassion for them?

Just now I visited a garden and the flowers that bloomed there will have withered by the evening. Their life is very short: they bloom in the morning and by the evening they are gone. When you remember the fact that these flowers that are smiling now will wither and fall and mix with the dust by evening, doesn't this fill you with compassion for them? Doesn't the idea that some of the stars in the night sky break off and fall fill you with compassion for the stars? If there were a deeper understanding, as we look at everything around us we would feel compassionate towards everything, we would feel very sympathetic towards everything. Our meeting is so short, this life is so difficult, this opportunity is so rare; so much passion, so many desires, so much pain inside each person...and still we are somehow living and loving and creating works of art – how much compassion might this not create?

A man once spat at Buddha. The man got so angry that he spat at him. Buddha wiped the spittle off and said to the man, "Do you want to say something more?"

Ananda, the disciple who was sitting with Buddha, said, "What are you talking about? Has he said anything? Just give me the order and I will take care of him. This is the limit, that he spits at you!"

But Buddha said, "He is trying to say something and he has no language for it. He is trying to say something and his language is powerless and his inner impulse is intense. He couldn't say it so he has said it through actions."

This I call compassion, that Buddha felt sympathy for the man because his language was so powerless. The man was trying to say something, he was trying to express something and he was very angry. He couldn't find the words so he expressed it by spitting. When someone comes to me with love and holds my hands, I feel so much compassion: he is trying to say something but language is inadequate. That person is trying to say something by holding my hands. When a person is hugging someone language is inadequate. Man is so helpless and he is trying to say something, so he brings his heart close to the other's because he cannot find another way.

Yesterday as I was leaving here some people started touching my feet, and I felt so much compassion. How helpless man is! He is trying to say something and he is not able to, so he touches the other's feet. One of my close friends was walking behind me; he is very rational and he said, "No, no! Don't do that!" He was also right. It is so sad what has happened to this world. The ones who are touching another's feet are authentic, but now there are people who want you to touch their feet. So in fact what he said was right: "No, no! Don't do that."

I found what he said to be both right and wrong. He was right when he said that it is wrong for anyone in this world to allow someone else to touch their feet, but it would also be a wrong world if there were no people left whose feet one might feel like touching. And it would also be a wrong world if there were no longer any hearts that could bow down at someone's feet. A world where we are not over-whelmed with feelings that can be expressed only by touch-ing someone's feet would be a sad world.

Do you understand what I am saying? – it would also be a sad world if we were never overwhelmed with feelings that could only be expressed by touching someone's feet. Man would become very dry, without meaning. And I have been amazed that when I see someone bowing down and touching my feet, I can see that he is not touching my feet, he is seeing something in my feet: for him, he is touching the feet of god-liness. I am reminding you of this. And up to now, whenever anyone has bowed down at someone else's feet – if he has been forced that is a different matter – but whenever he has bowed down he is really bowing to the feet of the divine. After all, what does anyone have in their feet that is worthy of bowing down to? But there are feelings inside which can be expressed in no other way.

Yesterday someone who loves me was in my room with me. In the evening, when I started to go for my shower, I switched on the light and he said, "Now that it is light, let me touch your feet."

I was really amazed! And he touched my feet and I saw

tears in his eyes. There is nothing more beautiful on earth than those tears. On this earth no poetry, no song is more beautiful than those tears, tears that come in a moment of love. And if you understand, if you remember, if you can see, how can you not be filled with compassion?

But what do you see? – you see things in people that don't give rise to compassion in you but to criticism. You are seeing in people what triggers your cruelty instead of your compassion. You are looking at the inauthentic in people, at what is not their heart but their helplessness.

A man swears at me – is this his heart? No, it must be his helplessness. There is a heart inside the worst of men, and if you are able to see it you will be filled with compassion, you will be filled with great compassion.

Buddha said on that morning, "I feel compassion, so much compassion. Language is so inadequate, Ananda. Man's heart is trying to say so much and it cannot manage it." He simply asked the man, "Would you like to say something more?"

What more could the man have said? Now it was difficult to say anything. The man left. In the night he repented so much that the next day he went to Buddha to apologize. He fell at Buddha's feet and started crying. Buddha said, "Ananda, do you see how inadequate language is? Now again he wants to say something and he is not able to. Yesterday he was trying to say something and he wasn't able to and he behaved in a certain way, and now again he is behaving in a certain way. Ananda, language is very inadequate and man deserves great compassion."

Life is short, just a few days. I am saying this as though it is just a few days long, but in reality not even the next few moments are a certainty. And if in these few moments of life we don't learn compassion for each other, we have not been human; we have not known life, we have not recognized it.

So spread compassion all around you. Look around you.– people are so unhappy, don't add to their unhappiness. Your compassion will lessen their unhappiness; just one word of compassion will lessen their unhappiness. Don't add to their unhappiness. You are all adding to each other's unhappiness; you are all helping each other to be more unhappy. Every single man has many people behind him making him unhappy. If an understanding of compassion is there, then you will change all the ways that you cause unhappiness in others. And if you can bring happiness to someone's life, you will find a way to do it.

Remember one thing: the one who brings unhappiness to others in the end becomes unhappy himself, and the one who brings happiness to others in the end reaches to the heights of happiness. That's why I am saying that someone who tries to give happiness develops the center of happiness inside himself, and someone who tries to bring unhappiness to others develops the center of unhappiness inside himself. The fruit does not come from the outside, the fruit is created within you. Whatever you do, you develop a receptivity for it inside yourself. Someone who wants love should give his love. Someone who wants bliss should start sharing his bliss. Someone who wants flowers to shower in his home should shower flowers in other people's homes. There is no other way. So compassion is an emotion that each person has to develop in order to enter into meditation.

The third key is joy, happiness, delight, a sense of bliss and a lack of anguish. You are all so full of anguish. You are sad and tired people; you are beaten people just dragging yourselves on the road of defeat to a bitter end. You walk as if you have already died. There is no energy, no life in your walk; there is no life in your day-to-day life. You are lethargic, sad, broken, defeated. This is wrong because however short life may be, however certain death may be, someone who has even a little understanding will not be sad.

Socrates was dying. He had been given the poison – and he was laughing! One of his disciples, Creto, asked him, "You are laughing and our eyes are filled with tears. Death is very near – this a time for sadness."

Socrates said, "Where is this sadness? If I die and I die completely, where is this sadness? There will be no one left to experience sadness. And if I die and I still remain, where is the need for sadness? What will be lost is not me; I am that which remains."

So he said, "I am happy. Death can do only two things: it can either completely destroy me, and if it completely destroys me I will be happy because I will not be there to experience sadness; and if part of me remains I will be happy because the part that is not me will have been destroyed. I will still remain. Death can only do two things, that's why I am laughing. "And, Socrates said, "I am happy because what can death take away from me? It will either completely annihilate me…but then what has it taken away from me? – because then the one it has taken from will also not be here. And if I remain, everything remains. If I remain then everything remains because that which was taken away was not me. This is why I say I am happy."

He is happy even as he faces death, and here you are, un-happy even to be alive. You are alive and still you are unhappy; yet there have been people who were happy even in the face of death.

Mansoor was tortured to death. His legs were cut off, his arms were cut off, they poked his eyes out. No one in history has been tortured more brutally. Christ was put to death quickly, Gandhi was killed quickly, with a bullet, Socrates was poisoned – but Mansoor is the one person who was put to the most painful death in history. First they cut off his legs, and when the blood started pouring out of his legs he took the blood and put it on his hands.

A large crowd had gathered around him; they were throw-ing stones at him. Someone asked him, "What are you doing?"

He said, "I am performing the *vaju*, washing my hands be-fore prayer." Mohammedans wash their hands before they pray. He washed his hands with his blood and he said, "I am performing the vaju." Then he said – remember these words of Mansoor – "The vaju of love, the real vaju of love, is done with blood, not with water. And only someone who performs the vaju with his own blood can enter into prayer."

People were at a loss. They thought he was mad. First his legs were cut off, then his arms were cut off, then they gouged out his eyes. Thousands of people had gathered: they were throwing stones at him and one by one his body parts were being cut off. And when they pierced his eyes he cried, "Oh God, remember that Mansoor has won."

And people asked, "What do you mean? What have you won?"

He answered, "I am asking God to remember that Mansoor

has won. I was afraid that in the midst of so much animosity and hatred, maybe love would not survive. God, remember that Mansoor has won – my love is unending. Whatever these people are doing to me, they haven't succeeded in destroying my love. They haven't been able to do what they are trying to do. This love is eternal." And he said, "This is my prayer, this is my worship."

Even then he was laughing! Even then he was drunk with the divine.

People have faced death laughing and happy, but you sit with long faces, sad and miserable even as you face life. This is a wrong way. A person who is full of enmity cannot go on the spiritual journey. For the spiritual journey cheerfulness is needed; for the spiritual journey you need a spirit full of bliss.

So be cheerful all the time. These are just habits – sadness is just a habit that you have formed. Cheerfulness is also a habit that you can form. To support cheerfulness you have to look at the aspects of life which are full of light, not darkness. If I tell you that I have a friend who sings very beautifully or plays the flute very beautifully, you will say, "Maybe – but how can this man play the flute when we have seen him drinking in the pub?" If I tell you that this friend plays the flute very beautifully you will say to me, "How can this be when we have seen him drinking alcohol in the pub?" This is supporting darkness. If I tell you, "This is my friend, he drinks alcohol," and you say to me, "Maybe so, but he also plays the flute very beautifully!" – this is looking on the bright side of life. Someone who wants to be happy will look on the bright side. Someone who wants to be happy will see that there is one night between two days, and someone who wants to feel miserable will see that there is one day between two nights.

The way we look at life has a direct affect on what develops inside us. So don't look at the dark side of life, look at the bright side of life.

When I was small my father was poor. With great difficulty he built himself a house. He was poor and he was also ignorant; he had never built a house before. He managed to build this house with great difficulty. He must have done it without knowing how to do it, because when it was finished, before we could move into it the rains came and it collapsed. I was small and I was very sad. My father was not in town, so I sent a message to him that the house had collapsed and all the hopes we had of moving into it had turned to dust.

When he arrived he distributed sweets to the people of the town! And he said, "I am very grateful to God. If the house had collapsed eight days later not a single child of mine would be alive." We were supposed to have moved into the house eight days later. After that, for his whole life he was happy about the fact that the house had collapsed eight days earlier. If it had collapsed eight days later it would have been a tragedy.

Life can be looked at in this way as well – so much joy and bliss arises in the life of someone who looks at it in this way. It all depends on how you look at life. Life has no meaning on its own: it all depends on how you look at it. Your attitude, your way of looking at it, your understanding is what makes it or breaks it.

Ask yourself what it is that you focus on. Have you ever

come across a person so evil that he does not possess even one saintly quality? And if you can find such a quality then focus on it – that is the real essence of the man. In life, look for radiance and for light everywhere because through this, radiance and light will be born within you. This is joyfulness.

The third feeling is to become filled with joy. You become so full of joy that it negates death and misery. You become so blissful that death and misery shrivel up and die; you don't even realize that death and misery exist.

A person who cultivates cheerfulness and bliss inside himself will make progress in his meditation. This is very, very important for the progress of meditation.

There was once a saint who was so happy with life that people were puzzled, because they had never seen him sad or in pain. When the time of his death came he said, "Now in three days I will be gone. And I am letting you know this so that you remember not to cry on the grave of a man who has laughed his whole life. I am letting you know this so that no sadness falls on this hut. It has always been blissful here, it has always been cheerful here. So make my death a celebration, don't make it into a reason for mourning. Don't mourn my death, make it into a celebration."

But the people became sad, they became very sad. He was such an amazing man and the more amazing he was the deeper was the sorrow of the people. There were many people who loved him. For three days they all started gathering around him, and until he died he was telling people jokes, making them laugh and talking to them with love. Then in the morning before he died he sang a song, and after finishing the song he said, "Remember, don't take off my clothes. Put my body with these clothes on the funeral pyre. And don't give me a bath!"

Those were his last instructions, and then he died. He was burned on the funeral pyre with his clothes on. And while he was burning on the funeral pyre and the people were standing around feeling sad, suddenly they were shocked. He had hidden fireworks and sparklers in his clothes, and when he was put on the funeral pyre the sparklers and fireworks started going off. His funeral pyre became a celebration! The people started laughing and said, "He made us laugh in his life, and he has also made us laugh in his death."

Life has to be transformed into laughter. Life has to be made a joy and even death has to be made a joy. And a person who succeeds in doing this will be blessed and filled with gratitude. A person who enters meditation in this space will move faster than one can imagine, he will become like an arrow.

Someone who enters meditation with a burdened mind has tied stones to the arrow – then how far will the arrow go? The faster you want to go the more carefree and light your mind needs to be. The farther you want the arrow to go, the lighter the arrow must be. And the higher you want to climb, the more luggage you will have to leave at the bottom. And the biggest burden is your misery, your sadness, your enmity. There is no bigger burden than this.

Have you watched people? – they walk as if they are being weighed down, as though they are carrying a heavy burden on their heads. Drop this burden and say yes to joy! Give a lion's roar of joy! Let the world know that no matter what kind of life you have, it can be made into a song, it can be filled with joy. Life can become music. Remember this third thing – joy.

And the fourth thing is gratitude: gratitude is divine. In this century, if anything has been lost it is gratitude.

Do you know that when you are breathing in it is not you who is breathing in? – because the moment the breath does not come in you will not be able to take it in. Are you sure that it was you who was born? No, it was not you. You did not play any conscious role in your birth, it was not your decision. Are you aware how amazing the small body that you have received is? It is the greatest miracle on earth. You eat a little food and this small stomach of yours digests it – this is a great miracle.

Science has advanced so much, but if we were to open up large factories and engage thousands of specialists it would still be difficult to digest a single chappati and turn it into blood. It is so difficult to digest a chappati and transform it into blood, and this body of yours is performing miracles twenty-four hours a day – this small body, a few bones, a little flesh. Scientists say that the body is made up of materials that would cost four or at the most five rupees. It is not made of costly materials. Such a great miracle is with you for twenty-four hours a day and you are not grateful to it!

Have you ever loved your body? Have you ever kissed your hands? Have you ever loved your eyes? Have you ever realized what an amazing thing is taking place? It is very unusual to find someone among you who has loved his eyes and who has kissed his hands, who has experienced gratitude that this amazing thing is happening without his knowledge and even without his participation.

So first of all be grateful to your body. Only someone who is grateful to his body can be grateful to other people's bodies. First of all become filled with love for your body, because only someone who is filled with love for his own body is capable of loving other people's bodies. The people who are teaching you to be against your body are irreligious. The people who are telling you that the body is your enemy, that it is evil, that it is this and that, are irreligious. The body is a great miracle. The body is amazingly helpful – be grateful to it.

What is this body? This body is made up of five elements – be grateful to the body, be grateful to these five elements.

What will happen to you if one day the sun dies? Scientists say that in four million years the sun will die: it has given enough light, it is becoming empty, and a day will come when it will die. Right now we are under the impression that the sun will rise every day. But a day will come when people will go to bed thinking that the sun will rise tomorrow and it will not rise. And then what will happen? Not only will the sun die, life itself will die because life is sustained by it, because all heat and energy are sustained by it.

You sit by the side of the ocean: have you ever thought that seventy percent of your body consists of ocean water? Man was born on land, but micro-organisms first came into existence in the ocean. And you will be surprised to know that even now the proportion of salt to water in your body is the same as in the ocean. And when this proportion in the body is slightly disturbed you get sick.

Sitting by the side of the ocean, do you ever remember that you also have something of the ocean inside you? You should be grateful to the ocean for the ocean which is inside you, and you should be grateful to the sunlight for the sun which is inside you, and you should be grateful to the wind which is moving your breath. You should be grateful to the sky and the earth that made you. This I call gratitude, divine gratitude.

You cannot become religious without this gratitude. How can an ungrateful man become religious? Once you begin to experience this gratitude constantly, you will be surprised – this gratitude will fill you with so much peace, with so much mystery. And then you will understand one thing: that you are not worthy of being given all these things, but because you have all these things you will be filled with thankfulness. You will be filled with gratitude because what you have received will give you a sense of fulfillment.

Express your gratitude. Find ways to develop gratefulness and your meditation will deepen through it. And not only your meditation, but your whole life will change tremendously. Your life will become very different, it will become something completely new.

Jesus was crucified and when he was dying he said, "Father, forgive them. Please forgive them because one, they don't know what they are doing" – that was his compassion – "and two, there was a distance between you and me, and now that gap has closed. They have helped me to drop the distance that was there between us. For that I am grateful to them."

So when you relate with anyone in your life, constantly remember your gratitude. You will find your life becoming full of wonder.

I have told you four things that are necessary for the purity of the emotions: friendliness, compassion, cheerfulness and gratitude. There are many other things, but these four are enough. If you meditate over them the rest will

145

automatically follow on their own. This is how the emotions will become pure.

I have told you how the body can be purified, how your thoughts can be purified and how emotions can be purified. Even if you can only manage these three you will still enter into a new and amazing world. Even if you manage only these three, much will happen.

I will talk about the three main principles later on. I will discuss emptiness of the body, emptiness of the mind and emptiness of the emotions. I have been talking about purification; later I will be talking about emptiness. And when purity and emptiness meet, *samadhi,* enlightenment happens.

Now we will sit for the morning meditation which I have already explained to you. We will begin by making the resolution five times. Then for a while we will go into the feeling state. Then we will watch the in-breath and the out-breath, keeping the spine erect, the eyes closed, watching with awareness the area near the nose where the breath comes in and goes out.

Everybody spread out so that no one is touching anyone else.

THE PATH OF MEDITATION

body and soul:
science and religion

Chapter 6

My Beloved Ones,

*t*HERE ARE some questions – in fact, there are many questions. I will try to give a combined answer to all of them. I have divided them into categories.

The first question is: *What is the place of religion in the scientific age? And what is the use of religion in national and social life?*

Science is the form of knowledge which looks for the inner, hidden power in matter. Religion is the form of knowledge which looks for the inner, hidden power in consciousness. There is no conflict between religion and science; in fact they are complementary to each other.

In an age which is only scientific there will be more conveniences, but there will not be more happiness. In an age which is only religious some people will know happiness, but mostly, people will suffer inconveniences. Science provides the conveniences, religion brings peace. If there are no conveniences, very few people can know peace. If there is no peace, then many people can acquire conveniences but they will not know how to enjoy them.

Until now all the civilizations that man has given birth to were incomplete, fragmented. The culture that the East gave birth to depended purely on religion. It was not interested in science. As a result, the East was defeated; it became impoverished and ruined. The culture that the West gave birth to is at the other extreme: it is based on science and it has nothing to do with religion. As a result, the West has triumphed and has accumulated wealth, prosperity and conveniences – but it has lost its soul.

The culture that will arise in the future, if it is truly to be for the evolution of mankind, will be a balance of science and religion. This culture will be a synthesis of religion and science. It will not be only religious or only scientific: it will be either scientifically religious or religiously scientific.

So far, both experiments have been failures. The Eastern experiment has failed and the Western experiment has also failed. But now we have an opportunity to create a universal experiment which is neither of the East nor of the West, in which both religion and science are combined.

So I say to you that there is no conflict between religion and science, in the same way that there is no conflict between the body and the soul. Anyone who lives only on the level of the body will lose his soul, and someone who tries to live only in the spiritual dimension will also not be able to live rightly because he will lose contact with his body.

Just as human life is a balance, a synthesis of body and soul, in the same way a complete culture would also be a balance, a synthesis between science and religion. Science would be its body, religion its soul.

But if somebody were to ask me that if we had to choose between religion and science, what should we choose? Then I would say that we should be ready to choose religion. If somebody were to ask me to choose between science and religion because one of them had to go, I would say be ready to choose religion. It would be better to be poor and inconvenienced than to lose the soul of man.

What is the value of conveniences that cost us the self? And what is the value of wealth that deprives us of our very being? In reality, they are neither conveniences nor wealth.

I will tell you a short story, it has always been one of my favorites.

I have heard that once a king in Greece fell sick. He was so sick that the physicians said he was not going to live, there was no hope. So his ministers and the people who loved him became very worried and anxious. Just then a fakir entered the village, and somebody said, "People say that if you call the fakir and he gives his blessings, sick people are cured."

They went to get the fakir and he came. The moment he came in he said to the king, "Are you crazy? Is this what you call a disease? It is not a disease. There is a very simple treatment for it."

The king, who had been lying in bed for months, sat up and said, "What treatment? I thought I was finished. I don't have any hope of getting better."

The fakir said, "It is a very easy treatment. Bring the coat of a man of the village who is both prosperous and peaceful, and this the king should wear. He will become healthy and well."

The ministers ran…. There were many prosperous people in the village. They went from house to house saying, "We want the coat of a man who is both prosperous and peaceful."

And the prosperous people said, "But we are unhappy….

A coat! – we can give our lives, what to say of a coat. If the king can be saved, we are prepared to give everything. But our coats won't work because we are prosperous, but we are not peaceful."

They went to each and every man in the village. They searched the whole day, and by the evening they had lost all hope. They realized that it was going to be difficult to save the king – a cure was beyond reach. In the morning they had thought, "The cure will be very easy to find," but by the evening they realized, "The cure is very difficult, in fact, impossible to find." They had been to all the rich people.

In the evening they returned, tired and sad. The sun was setting. Outside the village, near the river and sitting next to a rock, someone was playing a flute. Its sound was so musical and there were such waves of bliss arising from it that one of the ministers said, "Let's ask this last person…maybe he is peaceful."

They went to him and asked, "The sound of your flute, your song sounds so full of bliss and peace that we would like to ask you something. The king is sick and we need the coat of a man who is both peaceful and prosperous."

The man said, "I am willing to give my life, but just look closely…I don't have a coat." They looked closely, it was dark – the man who was playing the flute was naked.

So the king could not be saved because the man who was peaceful was not prosperous, and the ones who were prosperous did not have peace. In the same way, this world can't be saved because the cultures that have a legacy of peace don't have prosperity, and the cultures that are prosperous don't even think about peace. The king died.

Mankind will also die. The treatment that mankind needs is the same as what the king needed. We need the coat and we also need peace. Until now, our ideology has been incomplete. Until now we have thought about man in a very incomplete way, and we habitually move to the extremes. The human mind's greatest disease is its tendency to go to the extremes.

Confucius was staying in a village when somebody said to him, "There is a very scholarly and thoughtful man, would you like to meet him?"

Confucius said, "First let me ask you why you call him very thoughtful, and then I will definitely come to meet him."

The people said, "He is thoughtful because before doing anything he thinks three times – three times!"

Confucius said, "This man is not thoughtful; three times is a bit too much. Once is too little, twice is enough. An intelligent man stops in the middle, an ignorant man goes to the extremes."

The first point of ignorance is if a person thinks himself to be only the body. The second point of ignorance, and to the same degree, is if a person thinks himself to be only the soul. The individuality of man is a synthesis: the culture of man will also be a synthesis.

And it is time we learned our lesson. India's historical poverty and defeat, and the downtrodden state of all the

Eastern countries are not without a reason, and the reason is religious extremism. And the fact that Western countries have become poor from within is also not without a reason: the reason is scientific extremism. The future will be beautiful if science and religion are integrated. This much is clear: in the integration of religion and science, religion will be the center and science the circumference. It is clear that with the integration of science and religion, religion will necessarily be the intelligence and science its follower. The body cannot be the master; science also cannot be the master. Religion will be the master. And then we will be able to create a better world.

So don't ask about the use of religion in the scientific age. Religion is of genuine use in the scientific age because science is an extreme, and it is a dangerous extreme. Religion will give it a balance, and it will be able to save man from the danger of that extreme.

This is why the moment of the resurrection of religion all over the world is very close at hand. It is very natural – and it is absolutely certain. It is needed for there to be a resurrection of religion, otherwise science will only lead to death. So it is pointless to ask what need there is for religion in the scientific age: religion is *most* needed in this age of science.

Related to this, it has also been asked of what use is religion in national and social life.

I think that what I have just said might have answered this question as well, because something which is useful to the individual is most definitely going to be useful to the nation and society as a whole. After all, what is a nation and a society except a collection of individuals? So don't be under the illusion that a nation can live without religion.

This misfortune has happened in India. We misunderstood certain words; we started talking about a religionless state. We should have said a 'non-sectarian' state but we started talking about a religionless state. It is one thing to be a nonsectarian state, and a totally different thing to be a religionless state. Any intelligent person will be in favor of a non-sectarian state, but only a fool can be in favor of a religionless state.

To be non-sectarian means that we are not concerned with Jainism, Hinduism, Buddhism or with Mohammedanism. This is what it means to be non-sectarian. But to be a religionless state means that we are not concerned with truth, with non-violence, with love or with compassion. No nation can be religionless in that sense. And if it is, then that is its misfortune. The nation must make religion its very life-energy, and not be religionless. But yes, it is absolutely necessary to be non-sectarian.

The atheists in the world have not harmed religion very much; the scientists in the world have not harmed religion very much. The people who have harmed religion most are the religious leaders. They are the people whose emphasis is less on religion than on being a Jaina, whose emphasis is less on religion than on being a Hindu, whose emphasis is less on religion than on being a Mohammedan. These are the people who have deprived the world of religion. Sects which should have been the body of religion have proved to be its murderers. Religion has great value, but sects have no value. The fewer sects and sectarians there are, the better.

It is impossible for any race, any nation or any society to continue without the foundation of religion. How is it possible? Can we continue without the foundation of love? How can a nation be a nation without the foundations of love or truth? Or can a nation be a nation without the foundation of unselfishness, of non-possessiveness, of non-violence and fearlessness? These are the basic qualities of the soul. In their absence there is no nation, no society. And if there is such a nation, such a society, then anyone with even a little intelligence will see that it is a crowd of robots. It will be impossible to call it a nation.

A nation is formed through interrelationships – my relationship with you, and the relationships you have with your neighbors. All these interrelationships together become a nation. The more these relationships become based on truth, on love, on non-violence and on religiousness, the more fragrance there will be in the life of the nation, the more light there will be in the life of the nation and the less darkness there will be in the life of the nation.

So I say, the life of a nation and a society can only exist if it is founded on religion. You should be careful how you use this concept of secularism; the whole nation should be careful. Under the cover of this word there is great danger. Under the cover of this word you may believe that there is no need for religion. But religion is the *only* thing a human being needs. Everything else is secondary and can be dropped. Religion is something that cannot be dropped.

I think this will help you in solving your question.

Another friend has asked: *What should we meditate on?*

In general, with all the ideas that are around about meditation, you understand meditation to mean meditating upon something: you will meditate upon somebody or upon something. So naturally the question arises, on what to meditate? – who to pray to? who to offer your devotion to? who to love?

I told you this morning that there is one kind of love where I would ask you who you are in love with. And there is another kind of love where I would ask whether there is love inside *you* or not? It has nothing to do with the other.

There are two states of love: one in which love is a relationship, and the other in which love is a state. In the first love, if I tell you that I feel love you will ask, "For who?" And if I tell you that it is not a matter of someone, I just feel love, you will have trouble understanding. But it is this second state which has to be understood.

Only one who simply loves without the need for somebody to be there, really loves. What will someone who loves a particular person do about everyone else? – he will be filled with hatred towards everyone else. And what will someone who meditates on a particular person do about everyone else? – he will be filled with unconsciousness towards everyone else.

The meditation I am talking about is not a meditation *on* something: rather, it is a state of meditation. So this is what I mean when I am talking to you about meditation as a state. Meditation does not mean remembering someone. Meditation means to drop everything which is in one's memory and to come to a state where only consciousness remains, where only awareness remains.

If you light a lamp and remove all the objects surrounding it, the lamp will still go on giving light. In the same way, if you remove all objects from your consciousness, all thoughts, all imagination, what will happen? – only consciousness will remain. That pure state of consciousness is meditation. You don't meditate on somebody. Meditation is a state where only consciousness remains.

When only consciousness remains without an object, that state is called meditation. I am using the word 'meditation' in this sense.

What you practice is not meditation in the real sense; it is only a concept. But meditation will happen on its own through this. Try to understand that what you are practicing at night, exercises involving the *chakras,* and in the morning, exercises involving the breath, is all a discipline, it is not meditation. Through this discipline a moment will come when the breath will seem to have disappeared. Through this discipline a moment will come when the body seems to have disappeared and thoughts have also disappeared. What will remain when everything has disappeared? That which re-mains is meditation. When everything has disappeared, that which is left behind is called meditation. A discipline is *on* something; meditation is not *on* anything in particular. So what we are in fact doing is practicing the disciplines of the chakras and of the breath.

You will ask, "Wouldn't it be better if we practiced a dis-cipline using the idea of God? Wouldn't it be better if we practiced a discipline with an idol?"

That would be dangerous. It is dangerous because while you practice a discipline with an idol, the state which I am calling meditation will not happen. Practicing a discipline with an idol, there will only be the idol and nothing else. And the deeper the discipline goes with the idol, the more the idol will be there and nothing else.

It happened to Ramakrishna. He used to meditate on the mother goddess Kali; this was his discipline. Then slowly, slowly it happened that he started seeing Kali within himself. Closing his eyes, the idol became alive and he became very blissful, very joyous. But one day a sage came to see him. The sage said to him, "What you are doing is only imagination, it is not a meeting with God."

And Ramakrishna said, "It is not a meeting with God? But I see Kali alive!"

The sage replied, "Seeing Kali alive is not a meeting with God."

Some see a Kali, some see a Jesus, some see a Krishna – all these are fabrications of the mind. God does not have any visible form. The divine does not have a face, a manner, a shape. The moment consciousness enters the formless, it enters the divine.

You don't encounter the divine, you become one with it. There is no face-to-face encounter where you are standing on one side and God is standing on the other side. A moment comes when you merge with the infinite existence, just as a drop falls into the ocean. And the experience of that moment is the experience of the divine. You don't encounter or see God, you experience the merging with existence just as a drop feels when it falls into the ocean.

So the sage told him, "This is a mistake. It is only imagination." And he said to Ramakrishna, "Now, in the same way as you created this idol within you, cut it into two pieces. Raise an imaginary sword and smash the idol in two!"

Ramakrishna said, "Sword? Where will I find a sword?"

The sage said, "The way you create the idol is imagination. You can also imagine the sword and cut the idol with it. Let imagination destroy imagination. When the idol falls down nothing will be left behind. The world has already disappeared, and now only an idol remains – let go of that too. And when there is only empty space you will encounter the divine. What you are thinking is the divine is not the divine. This is a last barrier to God. Destroy that too!"

It was very difficult for Ramakrishna. He had meditated on this idol for years and nurtured it with so much love that it had started to appear to be alive. It was going to be very difficult to destroy it. He closed his eyes again and again but came back saying, "I cannot do this brutal act!"

But the sage said, "If you cannot do it, you cannot become one with the divine. Then your love for the divine is less than your love for the idol. Are you not ready to destroy an idol for the sake of the divine? Your love for the divine is not sufficient – you are not ready to get rid of an idol for it!"

You also don't have much love for the divine. You are also keeping idols between you and the divine – holding on to sects, holding on to religious scriptures – and you are not ready to let go of them.

The sage said, "You sit in meditation, and I will cut your forehead with a piece of glass. And when you feel me cutting your forehead with the piece of glass, gather some courage and cut Kali in two."

Ramakrishna found the courage, and when he had done it the idol had been cut in two. When he came back he said, "Today, for the first time, I have attained to *samadhi*. Today, for the first time, I have come to know what truth is. For the first time I am free of imagination and I have entered truth.

So this is why I am not asking you to imagine anything. I am not asking you to imagine something which will be an obstacle. And the few things that I have said about the chakras and about the breath are not an obstacle because you don't become infatuated with them. You are not concerned with them: they are only devices through which you can go within. They cannot become obstacles.

So I am only talking about using imagination in such a way that in the end it does not become a hindrance to your meditation. This is why I have not asked you to meditate *on* something, I have simply asked you to go into meditation. I have not asked you to *do* meditation, I have asked you to go into meditation.

You are not to meditate on something. You have to reach meditation within yourself. If you remember this, many things will become clear.

A friend has asked: *Why is spirituality overpowered by worldly interests, in spite of its being higher?*

Up to now, spirituality has not been overpowered. Up to today, the spiritual has never been overpowered by worldly interests. You will say that I am wrong because every day you must be feeling overpowered within yourself. But I ask you, do you have any genuine spiritual interest? What you are really saying is that what becomes overpowered does not exist in you; it is only an idea you have about spirituality, that you have heard about somewhere. If somebody tells you that diamonds outshine mere pebbles, what will you say? You will say that then they could not be real diamonds; the diamonds must be imaginary and the pebbles must be real. So of course the diamonds will be defeated and the pebbles will win. Because if the diamonds are real, then how can they be defeated by pebbles?

You must think that in your life your spiritual qualities are overpowered by your worldly interests. But where are those spiritual qualities? So whatever you think is being overpowered is only imaginary; the other part is just not present. You must be constantly thinking that hatred wins and love is overpowered. But where is love? You must think that the desire to attain money wins and it overpowers the desire to know the divine. But where is this desire to know the divine? If it is really there, no desire can overpower it. If it is really there, no other desire can even exist. The question of it being overpowered will not arise.

If someone were to say that there is light but it is overpowered by darkness, you would say that he is mad. If there is light, then darkness cannot enter. Until now there has been no war between light and darkness. Up to now there has never been a conflict between light and darkness because the moment there is light, darkness no longer exists. An opponent does not even exist, so winning is not an issue. Darkness can win only when light is not present at all, so it is victorious only in the absence of light. But there is no question of darkness in the presence of light because darkness disappears, it simply is not there.

What you are calling 'worldly interests' will disappear if spiritual interests happen in you. This is why my whole effort is to give more emphasis to creating a spiritual interest in you than to emphasize getting rid of your worldly interests. My emphasis is on the positive.

When a positive spiritual interest arises in you, your worldly interests become weak. When love arises within someone, hate disappears from within him. There has never been a collision between love and hate; up to now that has never happened. When truth arises within someone, lies disappear from within him. Truth and untruth have never been in conflict. When non-violence arises within someone, his violence disappears. Non-violence and violence have never yet been in conflict. It is not a question of defeat...there is not even a contest. Violence is so weak that the moment non-violence arises, it disappears. The non-spiritual is very weak, the world is weak, very weak.

This is why in India the world has been described as *maya*, illusion. Maya means something which is so weak that you just touch it a little and it disappears. It is magical. It is like someone showing you a mango tree that has just been conjured up, and as you get closer to it you find that it is not there. Or on a dark night you see a rope hanging and take it to be a snake; then as you come closer you find that there is no snake at all. The snake which you saw in the rope was an illusion: it appeared to be there but it was not.

That's why in India the world is said to be an illusion, because when anyone comes close enough, the moment he sees truth he will find that there is no world, as such. What you are calling the world has never encountered truth.

So when you feel that your spiritual interests are being defeated, realize one thing: these interests of yours must be imaginary. You must have learned them by reading books, they are not within you. There are many people....

A person came to me and asked, "In the past I used to experience God, but I don't anymore!"

I said to him, "It must never have happened. Is it possible that you start experiencing the divine and then you don't?"

Many people come to me and say, "I used to experience meditation but now I can't anymore."

I tell them, "It never happens like that, because it is impossible to have experienced meditation and then to have lost it."

Keep this in mind: in life, higher states can be reached but they can never be lost. You can reach to higher states but you cannot lose them, there is no way to lose them. You can become wise, you can attain wisdom, but you cannot lose it. It is impossible.

But what happens is that with education and with conditioning, some so-called religious feelings arise in you. You believe them to be religious, they are not religious, they are just conditioning. There is a difference between religiousness and conditioning. From childhood on, you are taught that there is a soul. You learn it, you cram it, you memorize it, it becomes a part of your memory system. And later on you still go on to saying that there is a soul and you think you *know* that there is a soul.

You don't know it at all. It is an idea that you once heard somewhere, a false thing which other people have taught you. You don't know anything at all. And then if this so-called soul is defeated by your passions, you say, "The soul is so weak that it is defeated by my desires." You don't have a soul, you just have an idea. And that idea has been created by the society , it is not yours. When the energy of spiritual interests awakens through your own experience, then worldly

163

interests disappear. They no longer have a hold on you.

Remember this: if you feel that you are being defeated, realize that what you have believed to be religion must have been what you thought religion was, not your own experience of religion. Somebody must have told you, you did not experience it yourself. You must have heard it from your parents. You may have got it from tradition, but it has not happened within you. You think there is light but there is none – that is why darkness wins. When there is light, its very presence defeats darkness. Light does not fight with darkness: its very presence, its very existence is the defeat of darkness.

Keep this in your mind, and throw out the empty, so-called spiritual interests and religious feelings that get defeated. Knowing them to be empty, they have no meaning. The understanding of how to create an authentic spiritual interest will come to you only when you have understood how to drop the false interests.

Many of you go on carrying the burden of totally imaginary things, things which don't exist. It is as though you are one of those beggars who thinks himself to be a rich man, which you are not. Why when you put your hand in your pocket and don't find any money, you ask, "What kind of wealth is this?" This is not wealth at all.

Beggars have a favorite pastime: dreaming about being rich – and all beggars dream of becoming rich. So the more worldly you are, the more you will dream about being religious.

There are many ways to dream. Go to the temple in the morning, donate a little something, perform some rituals, sometimes even read a little from the Gita, the Koran or the Bible, so the illusion is created that you are religious.

These acts create the illusion that you are religious. And then when these so-called religious interests are defeated by worldly desires, you become very sad and full of regret, and you think, "How weak spiritual interests are and how strong worldly interests are." But you don't have any spiritual interests. You are deceiving yourself by thinking that you are religious.

So you need to understand that a spiritual interest which can be defeated by sexual desire is false. This is the criterion: the spiritual interest which can be defeated by worldly interests is false. The day an interest is born in you in whose presence your worldly interests disappear – where even if you look for them you will not be able to find them – that day, something will have truly happened to you. You will have had a glimpse of religiousness.

If the sun rises in the morning and the darkness remains as it is, know that you are only dreaming that the sun has risen. When the sun rises, darkness disappears by itself. The sun has never met darkness; the sun does not know that something like darkness exists. And it will never be possible for it to know.

Until now the soul has not known that something like worldly desires exist. When the soul awakens, then desires are nowhere to be found. The two have never met. Remember this criterion; it will be useful.

One friend has asked: *Is austerity needed in meditation?*

What I am describing to you – purification of the body, purification of the thoughts, purification of the emotions;

emptiness of the body, emptiness of the mind, emptiness of the emotions – this is austerity.

And what do people think austerity is? If somebody is standing in the sun, they think that he is practicing austerity. If somebody is lying on a bed of thorns, they think that he is practicing austerity. If somebody is sitting hungry, that means that he is practicing austerity. Our ideas about austerity are very materialistic, very bodily. Austerity, to most people, means torturing the body. If somebody is hurting his body, then he is practicing austerity. In actual fact, austerity has nothing to do with hurting the body. Austerity is something absolutely unique; it is something quite different.

If somebody is fasting you think he is practicing austerity – but he is only dying of hunger. And I will even go so far as to say that he is not fasting, he is only going without food. Going without food, not eating anything, is one thing; fasting is something totally different.

An *upvaas*, a fast, means to be living in the presence of the divine. It means to be near one's soul. It means to be close to the soul. And what does it mean to go without food? To go without food means to be close to the body. These are two diametrically opposite things.

A hungry man is closer to the body than to the soul. In comparison, a person with a full stomach is less close to the body. A hungry man always thinks about hunger, his stomach and his body. His line of thought concerns the body. His preoccupation is with the body and with food.

If being hungry were a virtue, poverty would become something to be proud of. If staying hungry were something spiritual, the poor countries would be spiritual. But do you know that no poor country can be spiritual? At least it has never happened until now. A country can only become religious when it is rich.

You remember the days of the past when the countries of the East were religious, when India was religious, but those were days of great prosperity, great happiness and great affluence. Mahavira and Buddha were the sons of kings; all twenty-four Jaina *tirthankaras* were the sons of kings. This is not a coincidence. Why was a tirthankara never born in a poor house? There is a reason for it: austerity always begins in the middle of affluence. A poor person is closer to the body. A rich person starts becoming free of the body, in the sense that his bodily needs have been fulfilled and for the first time he starts becoming aware of new needs which are of the soul.

This is why I am not in favor of you staying hungry, or of making someone else go hungry, or of calling poverty spiritual. The people who say this are under an illusion and they are deceiving others as well. They are only supporting poverty and finding false ways to feel contented. Staying hungry has no value, fasting has value. Yes, it is possible that in the state of fasting you forget about food and go without it, but that is a totally different matter. Mahavira was practicing austerity. He was not staying hungry, he was fasting. Through fasting he was continuously trying to reach closer to the soul. In some moments when he was closer to the soul, then he would forget the presence of the body. These moments can be prolonged and one or two days, even a month can pass.

It is said about Mahavira that in twelve years of practicing austerity, he ate only on three hundred and fifty days. One or two months would pass when he did not eat. Do you think that if he had been hungry, two months would have simply passed? A hungry man would have died. But Mahavira did not die because he was not aware of his body during those periods. There was so much closeness, such a proximity to the soul, that he was not aware that the body was also there.

And it is a great mystery...if you become unaware of the presence of the body, it starts functioning according to a totally different system and it no longer needs food. Now it is a scientific fact that if you become completely unaware of your body, it will start working in a totally different system and it will not need much food. And the more a person enters into the spiritual world, the more it will become possible for him to receive subtle, very subtle energy from food which is not possible for an ordinary person. So when Mahavira was fasting, it was only because he was so close to the soul that he would forget all about food. This is how it could happen.

Once a religious man was with me, and he said to me, "I am on a fast today."

I said, "You must mean you are going without food, but not fasting!"

He said, "What is the difference between going without food and fasting?"

I said, "When you go without food, you stop eating food and you start meditating on food. Fasting means that you are no longer concerned with food; you are in communion with the soul and food is forgotten."

Fasting is genuine austerity. And going without food is hurting the body, suppressing the body. People who have an ego go without food; egoless people fast. Going without food fulfills the ego, that "I haven't eaten for so many days!"

You hear praise and joy all around you. The news that you are very religious spreads everywhere. Even a little pain to the body greatly fulfills the ego, so people with big egos agree to do this.

I am telling you clearly that these are the concerns of the ego. These are not religious interests and concerns. Religious people definitely fast, but they don't go without food. Fasting means that one is totally involved in the effort to come close to the soul. And when one starts coming closer to the soul, it happens that food is completely forgotten.And I tell you this emphatically that it is true in everything, not only in this but in every aspect of life.

Yesterday I was talking to you about sex and love…or it might be something else. A person who is busy suppressing sex will seem very religious to you, but in fact he is not religious at all. A religious person is someone who is involved in the development of love, because by being more loving sex will disappear by itself. As you come closer to the divine there will be many changes within the body. The way you see the body will be different, it will change.

Austerity is the science through which a person forgets that "I am the body" and comes to know that "I am the soul." Austerity is a matter of technique. Austerity is a technique. A bridge, a way through which a person forgets that he is the body, and the realization dawns in him that he is the soul.

But false austerities are going on all over the world and they have created many dangers. They satisfy the egos of a few egoists but do great harm to the understanding of the masses, because the masses then believe that this is real austerity, that this is real meditation, that this is real yoga. But they are neither meditations nor yoga.

And I will tell you something more: people who are interested in the suppression of the body in this way are simply neurotic. Also, the people who enjoy hurting their bodies are the same people who enjoy inflicting pain on someone else's body. The only difference is that the joy they would experience by inflicting pain on other people's bodies is experienced instead by hurting their own bodies. These are violent people. This is masochism, it is violence towards oneself.

And I also remind you that there are two kinds of instincts in man: one instinct is to live, the survival instinct; and you may not be aware that there is another instinct in him to die, the death instinct. If there were no death instinct in man, there could not be so many suicides all over the world. A latent death instinct is present within everyone – so both of these are present within you.

The death instinct can provoke a person to kill himself. He starts enjoying it, getting juice out of it. Some people commit suicide in one go and some do it very slowly, in installments. Those who do it very slowly, you say they are practicing austerity, and the ones who do it in one go are said to have committed suicide. But those who do it slowly seem to be practicing austerity!

Austerity is not suicide. Austerity has nothing to do with death, it is related to infinite life. Austerity is not interested in death but in attaining to a more total life.

So my vision of austerity is contained in the three keys that I have just told you about, and we will discuss three more keys later on. These six keys explain what austerity is according to my vision. A person who enters into these six sutras is practicing austerity. Do you ever wonder whether it is really austerity when a person runs away and leaves his wife behind? People call this austerity...they will even call him a *sannyasin!* And yet it is possible that he has run away and left the wife behind but is still thinking about her. Austerity is when the wife is sitting next to you and you are not distracted by her. It is not austerity to run away and to still keep thinking about her.

And remember, the people who run away and leave things behind still go on thinking about those things. It is impossible for them not to, because if they were the kind of people who didn't they would be able to not think about them even as they remain with them.

Let me also tell you this: when things are present you don't think about them, but when they are not present any-more you start thinking about them. Have you not experi-enced this yourself? You don't think about what is in front of you, you think about what is absent. If the people you love are close to you, you forget about them; when they are far away you start remembering them. The farther away they are, the more intensely you remember them. You have no idea how much these so-called sannyasins suffer.

If all these religious people in the world were honest, then this illusion of their being religious would disappear. And if they were to truthfully expose their inner turmoil, what is happening in them and the agony they are going through, the longings they are suffering from, the desires which are giving them pain and the devil who seems to be tormenting them – if they were to tell you all this, you would realize that hell is right here on earth. I am saying this to you with authority: hell cannot be anywhere else in the world. A person's life is hell if he has not transformed his desires but has run away from them.

Austerity does not mean running away from anything, it is a transformation. Austerity is not renunciation but trans-formation. Austerity is not sacrifice, it is right-transformation – and whatsoever happens in that transformation is right. And whatsoever happens by running away, by renunciation, is not right. It will be very helpful if you can understand this.

Thousands of people are suffering. They have only one joy: of satisfying the ego. This also only a few people are able to satisfy, not all. The egos of people who are very intelligent, for some reason, are satisfied more easily. The rest only suffer and go on hoping that one day they will go to heaven, that they will be saved from going to hell and perhaps experience nirvana. The greed that is clinging to you is also clinging to them. And greed gives you the capacity to tolerate much pain. Even an ordinary man in his greed can tolerate more pain. An ordinary man who is greedy for money goes through so much pain to accumulate money, and people who are greedy to go to heaven also tolerate much pain.

When the people were taking Christ to crucify him, one of his followers asked, "We have given up everything for you: tell us, how will we be treated in the kingdom of God?" He asked, "We gave up everything for you, what will be our place in the kingdom of God?"

Christ must have looked at him with great pity and per-haps out of pity or jokingly, I don't know why he said it, he replied, "For you too there will be a place next to God."

The man became happy. He said, "Then it is okay."

Now would you say that this man has renounced? It is difficult to find a more greedy person than one who asks, "I gave up everything, now what will I get up there in return?" Someone who is thinking about getting something in return has not renounced at all. That is why all this talk of austerity – everyone talking about austerity – also gives you the entice- ment to practice a particular austerity, so that you will get a particular reward.

Austerity done with the desire to get something in return is false, because that is not austerity at all, it is a form of greed. This is the reason why all the existing forms of auster- ity promise you something in return. They tell you that all the people who practiced this or that austerity in the past at- tained to something or other. These are all forms of greed.

The only austerity is to try to know oneself. It is not that you will get a place in heaven through this or that – but you will experience great joy. Not to know one's own self is not to know life itself, and not to know your own self…. It is im- possible that the longing to know oneself does not arise in someone who has even a little intelligence. He will insist on knowing who he is and on becoming acquainted with the life-energy within him.

Austerity is the way to know the truth of life. Austerity is not a repression of the body. Yes, it is possible that many things which are happening to the meditator may seem to you to be a repression of the body, although he is not doing any such thing.

Have you ever seen a statue of Mahavira? When you look at his statue, do you feel that this man has repressed his body? Where else have you ever seen a body like this? And then have you looked at the saints who follow Mahavira? The moment you look at them you know that they have repressed their bodies. Their vital sources are all dried up. Their bodies are sad and dull, and their state of consciousness is also dull. They are only moving under the

173

spell of greed: "Where is the bliss, where is the peace that we can see in Mahavira's statue?"

This is something to think about. Mahavira dropped his clothes. You think he dropped his clothes because he thought that clothes should be renounced. No, he simply came to know the joy of being naked. I want to tell you very clearly that Mahavira did not drop his clothes because there was some joy in renouncing them, he dropped them because of the joy of being naked. Being naked was so blissful for him that wearing clothes became a disturbance. He found so much bliss by being naked that the presence of clothes became disturbing, so he threw away his clothes.

When a monk who is following him drops his clothes, he does not feel any joy in it. In fact, it is difficult for him to drop his clothes. And by going through that difficulty he thinks that he is practicing austerity. As he drops his clothes he thinks, "I am practicing austerity."

This was not austerity for Mahavira, it was an act of joy. And if somebody is following Mahavira without understanding him, without understanding his soul, he will only drop his clothes, and because dropping his clothes will be difficult for him, he will call this an austerity.

Austerity is not painful. There can be no greater joy than austerity. Yet those who practice it only superficially will feel that it is difficult and painful. And in exchange for going through so much pain they will satisfy their egos on the earth and will satisfy their greed for the other world. I don't call this austerity. Austerity is the process of entering within yourself with the help of the mind and body. And to enter into oneself is difficult and arduous – it takes great determination.

Think about this. If I am continuously standing in the

rain and the hot sun: is there more austerity in this than in the fact that when somebody abuses me, I don't become angry? Is there more austerity in lying on a bed of nails than in the fact that when somebody hits me with a stone, even the thought of hitting him back with a stone does not arise in my heart? Which one contains more austerity?

Anybody in the circus can lie on a bed of nails; standing in the hot sun is only a matter of practice, and after practicing it for a few days it no longer has any significance. It is very simple, it is absolutely simple. Remaining naked is a matter of practice. In fact, all the primitive people in the world live naked. But we don't call that austerity, and we don't go to them and fall at their feet as though they were doing something great. We know that it is their custom. It is very natural for them, it is not difficult for them.

Austerity does not mean that you just go on practicing something. But ninety-nine out of a hundred people are doing this. You will rarely come across someone whose austerity is the fruit of his joy – and austerity is true only when it is the fruit of joy. But when it is in the service of suffering it is nothing more than a form of masochism – it is not religious, it is neurotic.

And if understanding grows in the world, we will send this so-called religious person to a mental hospital, not to a temple. The time is not far away when someone who gets pleasure out of hurting his own body will need to be treated. And if someone is only enjoying the pleasures of his body he is also sick, just as someone who is getting joy out of hurting his body is sick on the other extreme. If someone is getting joy out of only using his body for pleasure, it is a sickness. It is the sickness of a person who is always looking for bodily pleasure. And if someone enjoys hurting his body, this too is a sickness – it is the sickness of the ascetic who has repressed all his bodily desires.

Someone who uses the body rightly becomes free of sickness. He is not identified with his body, either through indulgence or repression. The body is simply a vehicle. Only a person who is neither repressing the body nor indulging in it, whose pleasure or suffering is not dependent on the body, whose joy is not dependent on the body but rather on the soul – only such a person is moving towards religion.

There are two types of people whose joy is dependent on the body: one type who experiences joy by overeating, and the other type who experiences joy by not eating. But both are getting joy out of torturing the body – if they experience any joy, it is confined to the body. This is why I call both the person who indulges and this kind of religious person, materialistic: they are only concerning themselves with the body. For religion to be something that is only concerned with the body is very damaging. The spiritual qualities of religion need to be re-established.

One more question on this subject: *What is the difference between rag, desire; virag, renunciation of desire; and veetrag, beyond desire.*

Rag means attachment to something, *virag* means going against that attachment, and *veetrag* means beyond attachment.

If you try to understand what I was saying just now, then rag is the attachment to something and virag is the denial of that attachment. If a person accumulates money it is rag, and if someone renounces money and runs away, this is virag. But the focus in both cases is money. The person who is accumulating is thinking about money, and the person who is leaving it behind is also thinking about money. One is getting joy from having accumulated so much – he has so much and his ego is satisfied by thinking about it – while the other is satisfying his ego by thinking about the fact that he has renounced so much.

You will be surprised…the people who have money keep an account of how much they have, but the people who have renounced money also keep an account of what they have renounced. These monks and religious people have lists of how many fasts they have done! They keep track of the different kinds of fasts they have done. Just as there is a record of renunciation, there is also a record of indulgence. Rag keeps a record, and virag also keeps a record, because their focal point is the same; they are holding onto the same thing.

Veetrag, to be beyond attachment, is not the same as virag, the denial of attachment. Veetrag is to be free of both attachment and the denial of attachment. Veetrag is the state of consciousness where there is neither attachment nor non-attachment. He is neutral. He has money but he is unconcerned.

Kabir had a son, Kamaal. Kabir was in the habit of virag, the denial of attachment. He did not like Kamaal's way, because if someone presented something to Kamaal he would keep it. Kabir told him many times, "Don't accept gifts from anyone. We don't need any money."

But Kamaal would say, "If money is useless, then what is the need then even to say no? If money is useless, then we don't ask for it because it is useless. But if someone comes here to unburden himself, why say no to him? After all, it is useless."

Kabir didn't like it. He said, "I want you to live separately."

His virag, his denial of attachment, was being shattered by it. So he told Kamaal to live separately, and Kamaal started living in a separate hut.

The king of Kashi used to go to visit Kabir. He said, "I don't see Kamaal around."

Kabir said, "I don't like his ways, his behavior is shallow. I have separated from him. He lives separately."

The king asked, "What is the reason?"

Kabir said, "He is greedy about money. Someone offers something and he takes it."

The king went to see Kamaal and, bowing down, placed a very valuable diamond at his feet. Kamaal said, "What did you bring? Just a stone!"

The king thought, "But Kabir said that Kamaal is attached to wealth, and he says that I have only brought a stone!" So he picked it up and began to put it back into his pocket.

Kamaal said, "If it is a stone, then don't bother to carry the burden back with you; otherwise you will still be thinking that it is a diamond."

The king thought, "There is something tricky going on." But he said, "So where should I put it?"

Kamaal replied, "If you are asking where to put it, then you don't consider it to be just a stone. And you *are* asking where to put it, so you don't think it is only a stone. Simply throw it away! What is the need to keep it?"

The king put it into a corner in the thatched roof of the hut. Then he left thinking, "This is cheating! When I turn my back it will be gone."

After six months he returned and said, "Some time ago I presented you with something."

Kamaal said, "Many people present things. And only if I have any interest in those gifts do I bother to either keep them or return them. But I have no interest in those gifts, so why should I keep track of them? Yes, you must have given me something. Since you are saying so, you must have brought a gift."

The king said, "My gift was not so cheap, it was very valuable. Where is the stone that I gave you?"

Kamaal said, "That is very difficult. Where did you put it?"

The king went and looked in the corner where he had stuffed it, and the stone was still there. He was surprised! This opened his eyes.

This man Kamaal was unique: for him it was only a stone. This is what I call veetrag, going beyond attachment. It is not virag, denial of attachment. This is to go beyond attachment.

Rag is an interest in holding on to something, and virag is to be interested in renouncing the same thing. Veetrag means that it has lost all meaning. Veetrag, going beyond desire, is the goal.

Those who attain to it know the ultimate bliss because all their attachment to the outside has dissolved.

And now, the last question: *Is meditation impossible without what you have called the foundation for meditation: purity of the body, purity of thoughts and purity of emotions?*

No, without them meditation is also possible, but it is possible only for a very few people. If you enter into meditation with total determination, then even without purifying any of these you can enter into meditation because the moment you enter, all of them will become pure. But if it is not easy for you to have so much determination – it is very difficult to have so much determination – then you will have to purify them one by one.

You will not attain to a state of meditation by making them pure, but you will attain to greater determination by making them pure. By purifying them, the energy which was wasted through impurity will be saved, and that energy will be transformed into determination. Then you will enter into meditation. Purifying these three is helpful, but not essential.

Purifying these three is essential for anyone who finds it impossible to enter into meditation directly, and who will otherwise not be able to enter into meditation. But they are not absolutely essential because if there is total determination, even for a moment, you can enter into meditation. Even for a moment, if someone gathers his total energy and takes the jump, then there is nothing that can stop him, no impurity can stop him. But only a few people have been fortunate enough to gather that much energy; only a few people have been fortunate enough to gather that much courage.

Only the kind of people that I am about to tell you about in this story can gather that much courage.

Once there was a man who thought that the world must end somewhere, so he set out to find the place where the world ends. He traveled thousands of miles, and kept asking people, "I have to find the place where the world ends."

Finally he came to a temple where there was a sign on which was written: Here Ends the World. He became very afraid...the sign had appeared; a little further and the world would end. And below the sign this was written: Do Not Go Any Further. But he wanted to see the end of the world, so he went on.

A short distance from there the world came to an end. There was a shoreline and below it an infinite abyss. He just had a look and he was scared to death. He ran back; he could not even look behind him because there was such an abyss. Chasms which are not so deep are scary, but they have a bottom; this one was infinite – it was the end of the world. The abyss was the end and there was nothing beyond the abyss. In his fear he ran into the temple and said to the priest, "This final point is very dangerous."

The priest replied, "If you had jumped, you would have seen that the end of the world is the beginning of godliness." He said, "If you had jumped into that abyss you would have found the divine."

But to gather enough courage to jump into the abyss, if you don't already have it, some preparation for meditation is needed. Only a person who is ready to jump into the abyss needs no preparation. And how can there be any preparation? There can be no preparation, and this is why I have called these preparations the external disciplines. They are the external means and they will help you up to a point. Anyone who has the courage can jump in directly, and whoever does not have the courage can use these steps, remember this.

Only these questions can be discussed today. The rest we will discuss tomorrow.

THE PATH OF MEDITATION

the light of consciousness

Chapter 7

My Beloved Ones,

HAVE SPOKEN about the outer aspects that are the foundations for meditation. Now I will talk about the central nature of meditation.

The basic foundation of meditation is to purify and experience the true nature of the body, the thoughts and the emotions. If even only this much happens your life will become very blissful. If even only this much happens your life becomes divine. If even only this much happens you will become connected with the beyond. But it will only be a meeting with the beyond, you have not yet merged with it. You have become connected with the beyond but have not yet become one with it. You are acquainted with the divine but you are not it. The foundation of purification will turn you towards the divine and focus your eyes on it, but it is the state of emptiness alone that will allow you to merge with the divine and become one with it.

In the beginning, at the periphery you come to know truth, at the center you become truth. So now I will talk about this second stage. I have called the first stage purification; I am calling this second stage emptiness. There are also three stages of this emptying: at the level of the body, the mind level and the emotional level.

Bodilessness is the opposite of identification with the body. You are identified with the body. You don't feel "It is my body"; on the contrary, on some level you go on feeling that "I am the body." If the feeling that you are the body disappears, then you will become bodiless. If your identification with the body is broken, bodilessness will happen.

When Alexander was returning from India he wanted to take a *sannyasin* back with him so that he could show people in Greece what an Indian sannyasin looks like. There were many sannyasins who were ready and eager to go. Who wouldn't want to go when Alexander was inviting and greeting them with royal honors? But Alexander did not want to take just anyone who was eager, because one who was eager would not be a true sannyasin. He was looking for a sannyasin who had some authenticity.

When he was crossing the border regions, he found out about one particular sannyasin. People told him, "There is a sannyasin who lives on the bank of the river in the forest. You should take him with you."

He went there. First he sent his soldiers to bring the sannyasin to him. The soldiers went to the sannyasin and said, "You are fortunate! Thousands of other sannyasins have begged Alexander to take them but he did not choose any of them. Now the great Alexander has showered his favor on you and he wants you to go with him. You will be taken to Greece in royal style."

The sannyasin said, "Nobody has the power or the courage to force a sannyasin to go anywhere."

The soldiers were shocked. They were the soldiers of the mighty Alexander, and a naked sannyasin dared to talk to them like this? They said, "Don't say that again, or you will lose your life."

But the sannyasin said, "Nobody can take away a life that I have already dropped on my own. Go and tell your Alexander that his power may conquer everything, but it cannot conquer those who have already conquered themselves."

Alexander was amazed! The words were strange, but significant too because he felt that he had found the sannyasin that he had been searching for. Alexander himself went, naked sword in hand, and he told the sannyasin, "If you don't come, I will cut off your head."

And the sannyasin answered, "Do it! And just as you will see that you have cut the head off this body, I also will see that the head has been cut off the body. I will also see it, I will also be watching this happening. But you will not be able to kill *me,* because I am the watcher." And he went on, "I also will see that the head has been cut off – so don't be under the wrong impression that you can hurt me in some way. I am beyond the point where anyone can hurt me."

This is why Krishna has said, "That which fire cannot burn, which an arrow cannot pierce, which a sword cannot cut, that is-ness, that being is within us. The integrated being which fire cannot burn and an arrow cannot penetrate is within us."

The awareness of that being and the dropping of the identification with the body, the dropping of the feeling that you are the body, is bodilessness. But you will have to do something to drop the identification. You will have to learn how to drop it. And the more pure the body is, the more easy it will be to drop the identification with the body. The more the body is in a state of purity, the more quickly you can become aware that you are not the body. This is why body purity is the basis and bodilessness is its ultimate fruit.

How can you learn that you are not the body? You will have to experience it. If standing, sitting, sleeping and waking you try to remember, if there is a little right-mindfulness, if there is a little awareness of the functions of the body, you will have taken the first step towards creating emptiness.

When you are walking along a path, look deeply inside yourself and you will see that there is someone in there who is not walking. You are walking, your hands and feet are moving, but there is something within you which is not walking at all, which is just watching you walk.

When you have some pain in your hand or foot, when you have hurt your foot, then look inside with awareness – are *you* hurt, or is it that your body is hurt and you are getting identified with the pain? When there is some pain in the body become aware if the pain is happening to *you* or whether you are simply witnessing the pain, whether you are a witness to the pain.

When you feel hungry, look with awareness to see if you are hungry, or your body is hungry and you are simply witnessing this. And when there is happiness, also watch and feel where this happiness is actually happening.

With all that is happening in your life, while you are standing, sitting, walking, sleeping and waking, what needs to be remembered is to be aware to make a constant effort to see where things are actually happening. Are they actually happening to you or are you just a witness?

187

Your habit of identification is deep. You may even start to cry while you are watching a movie or a play, you may start to laugh. When the lights in the theater come on you secretly wipe away your tears so that nobody sees them. You cried, you became identified with the movie. You became identified with the hero, the character – something painful may have happened to him, and you identified with this pain and started to cry.

A mind which thinks that whatever is happening to the body is happening to you is in misery and pain. And there is only one cause for all your misery, and that is your identification with the body. And there is also only one cause for happiness, and that is that your identification with the body breaks and you become aware that you are not the body.

For that, right-remembrance is needed. Right-remembrance of the activities of the body, right-awareness, right-observation of the activities of the body are needed. It is a process: bodilessness will happen through right-observation of the body.

It is necessary to observe the body. When you go to bed at night, it is important to be aware that your body is going to bed, not you. And in the morning when you get out of bed, it is important to be aware that your body is getting out of bed, not you. It was not you that has slept, it was only your body that slept. When you eat, be aware that your body is eating, and when you wear clothes be aware that the clothes only cover the body, not you. Then when somebody hurts you, with this awareness you will be able to remember that the body is being hurt, not you. In this way, with constant reminders, at some point there will be an explosion and the identification will be broken.

Do you know that when you are dreaming you are not aware of your body? And do you know that when you are in deep sleep you remain unaware of your body? Do you remember your face? The deeper you go within yourself, the more you forget your body. In a dream you are not aware of your body; and in very deep sleep, in a state of unconsciousness, you are not aware of the body at all. When consciousness starts returning, your identification with the body gradually starts to return. In the morning, when you suddenly wake up, look inside, and you will clearly be able to see that your identification with the body is also waking up.

There is an experiment to break this identification with the body. If you go on doing it once or twice a month, it will help you to break the identification. Now try to understand this experiment.

Relax the body in the same way as we did for the night meditation: by making the room dark, giving suggestions to each *chakra*, relaxing the body, and entering into meditation. When the body is relaxed – when your breathing has become relaxed and your being has becomes silent – feel as if you have died. And become aware within yourself, since you are dead, which of your loved ones are gathering around you. Watch their images gathering around you – what they do, which of them cries, who screams, who grieves – watch them with great clarity; they will be visible to you.

Then see that all the people from the neighborhood, the locality, as well as all your loved ones have gathered and tied your dead body onto the bier. Watch that also. See the people carrying the bier, and let it reach the cremation ground; then let them put it on the funeral pyre.

Watch all this. All this is imagination, but if you experiment with all this in your imagination you will be able to see it very clearly. And then see that they have put your dead body on the funeral pyre; the flames have risen and your dead body has disappeared.

When your imagination reaches the point where the dead body has disappeared and the smoke has risen into the sky, the flames have disappeared into the air and only ashes are left, immediately, with total awareness, look inside yourself at what is happening. At that moment you will suddenly find that you are not the body; at that moment the identification will be totally broken.

After doing this experiment many times, when you get up after doing it, when you walk, when you talk, you will know that you are not the body. We have called this state the bodiless state. Someone who comes to know himself through this process becomes bodiless.

If you do this all the time, for twenty-four hours a day – walking, getting up, sitting down, talking and remaining aware that you are not the body – then the body will be just an emptiness. And to know that you are not the body is rare. It is absolutely rare, nothing is more precious than this. To become disidentified with the body is absolutely rare.

After your body, your thoughts and your emotions have been purified, if you do this experiment with bodilessness, it will happen. And then many changes will start to happen in your life. All your mistakes, all your unconscious acts are connected to the body. You have not made one mistake or done one wrong act which was not connected to the body. And if you become aware that you are not the body, there is no longer any possibility for misery in your life.

Then if somebody stabs you with a sword you will see that he has cut your body with the sword, and you will be aware that nothing has happened to *you*. You will remain untouched. At that moment you will be like a lotus leaf in the water. The moment you become aware of your bodilessness your life will become peaceful, undisturbed. Then any outside events, any thunder or storms will not touch you because they can touch only the body. Their impact is only on the body; they affect only the body. But you think, mistakenly, that the impact is on you – this is why you suffer and feel pain or happiness.

This is the first stage of spiritual discipline: you learn to become free from the body. It is not difficult to learn, and those who make the effort will definitely experience it.

The second element of spiritual discipline is freedom from thoughts. Just as I said that bodilessness happens through the right-observation of the body, freedom from thoughts happens through the right-observation of your thoughts. The basic element of spiritual discipline is right-observation. In these three stages you have to look with right-awareness and right-observation at the body, the mind and the emotions.

Become an observer of the currents of thought that flow through your consciousness. Just like someone sitting by the side of a river watching the river flow by, sit by the side of your mind and watch. Or just as someone sits in the forest and watches a line of birds flying by, just sit and watch. Or the way someone watches the rainy sky and the moving clouds, you just watch the clouds of thoughts moving in the sky of your mind. The flying birds of thoughts, the flowing river of thoughts…in the same way, silently standing on the bank, you simply sit and watch. It is the same as if you are sitting on the bank, watching the thoughts flowing by. Don't do anything, don't interfere, don't stop them in any way. Don't repress in any way. If there is a thought coming don't stop it, if it is not coming don't try to force it to come. You are simply to be an observer.

In that simple observation you will see and experience that your thoughts and you are separate – because you can see that the one who is watching the thoughts is separate from the thoughts, different from them. And as you become aware of this, a strange peace will envelop you because you will not have any more worries. You can be in the midst of all kinds of worries but the worries will not be yours. You can be in the midst of many problems but the problems will not be yours. You can be surrounded by thoughts but you will not *be* the thoughts.

And if you become aware that you are not your thoughts, the life of these thoughts will begin to grow weaker, they will begin to become more and more lifeless. The power of your thoughts lies in the fact that you think they are yours. When you are arguing with someone you say, "My thought is…" No thought is yours. All thoughts are different from you, separate from you. You just be a witness to them.

I will tell you a story so that you understand this more deeply. It happened to Buddha….

A prince had been initiated, and on the very first day he went to beg for alms. He begged for food at a door where Buddha had told him to go. He received the food, ate and returned. But when he went back he said to Buddha, "Forgive me, but I will not be able to go there again."

Buddha asked, "What happened?"

He said, "When I went, I had to go two miles, and on the way I thought of the food I would like to eat. And when I got to the door, the *shravika*, a lay follower of Buddha had prepared this very food. I was surprised. Still, I thought it was a coincidence. But then it happened that when I sat down to eat, the thought came to my mind that when I was at home I used to rest for a few minutes every day. And I thought: who will ask me now if I would like to rest today? And just as I was thinking this, the shravika said, 'Brother, if you would stay for a while after you have eaten and rest, I would be obliged and grateful, and my house would be purified.'

"I was really surprised – but then again I thought it must be a coincidence that the thought came to my mind and she also mentioned it. So I lay down and was about to rest when the thought came to my mind: today I have no bed of my own and no shelter of my own; today I am under someone else's roof, lying on someone else's mat. And at that moment the shravika said from behind me, 'Oh monk, the bed is neither yours nor mine; and the shelter is neither yours nor mine.' Then I became afraid!

"It was difficult to believe that these coincidences could happen again and again, so I said to the shravika, 'Do my thoughts reach you? Are you aware of the thought-waves arising in me?' And the shravika answered, 'Meditating continuously, my thoughts have disappeared, and now I can see other people's thoughts.' Then I got really scared and came running here to you. Please forgive me, but I will not be able to go there again tomorrow."

Buddha asked, "But why not?"

And he answered, "Because...how can I say it? Forgive

me, just please don't ask me to go there again."

But Buddha insisted so he had to tell him: "Seeing this beautiful woman, some lustful thoughts arose in me – and she must also have been able to read these thoughts. Now how can I face her? How will I be able to stand at her door? I cannot go there again."

But Buddha said, "You will simply have to go there. It is part of your meditation. Only in this way will you become aware of your thoughts."

He was helpless…he had to go there the next day. But the next day it was not the same man who went there. The first time he had walked along the path asleep: he had not been aware of what thoughts were going through his mind. The next day he went with awareness, because now there was fear. He went there consciously. And when he arrived at her door, he waited for a moment before climbing the steps. He made himself aware and he focused his awareness inwardly. Buddha had said, "Just look inside and don't do anything – simply be aware that no thought is unseen. Simply be aware that no thought passes you without your seeing it."

He climbed up the steps, watching within himself. He could almost see his breathing. He could even see the movement of his hands and feet. And as he ate, he was aware of each and every bite. It was as if someone else was eating the food and he was simply watching.

When you start to watch yourself there will be two currents within you: one which is doing and one which is only watching. There will be two parts within you: one is the doer and one is only a watcher.

He was eating his food, yet there was one person eating the food and someone else watching. In India we say – and

194

all the people in the world who have known say – "The one who is watching is you, and the one who is doing is not you."

He watched. He was surprised! He returned to Buddha dancing and he said to him, "This is great! I have discovered something. I have had two experiences: one experience is that when I am totally aware, thoughts stop. When I look inside with total awareness, thoughts stop. The second experience is that when the thoughts stop I see that the doer is different from the watcher."

Buddha said, "That is the key. And the one who finds it has found everything."

Become a watcher of your thoughts, but not a thinker – remember, not a thinker but a watcher of thoughts.

This is why we call our sages seers, not thinkers. Mahavira is not a thinker, Buddha is not a thinker; they are seers, watchers. A thinker is a sick person. People who don't know, think. People who know don't think, they watch. They are able to see it, it is visible to them. And the way to see is by observing the thoughts within you. Standing, sitting, sleeping or awake, watch whatever current of thought is flowing through you and don't get identified with any thought as though you were it. Let your thoughts flow separately from you and you be separate from them.

There should be two currents within you. An ordinary man who only thinks has just one current. A meditator has two currents within him, thoughts and watching. A meditator has two parallel currents within him, thoughts and witnessing.

An ordinary man has one current within him, that of thought. And an enlightened person also has only one current within him, that of simply watching. Try to understand this: an ordinary man has one current of thought within him, the watcher is asleep; the meditator has two parallel currents within him, thought and watching. Within an enlightened person only one current remains, that is watching. Thinking has died.

But because you have to learn watching from a state of thinking, you will have to meditate on thought and watching side by side. If we have to move from thought to watching, we will have to meditate on thought and watching simultaneously. This is what I call right-observation; this is what I call right-remembrance. Mahavira has called it 'wakeful intelligence'; mindfulness and wakeful intelligence. The one who is watching the thoughts is your wakeful intelligence. It is very easy to find thinkers, but it is difficult to find someone whose intelligence is awake.

Awaken your intelligence. I have told you how to awaken it – by watching your thoughts with awareness. If you watch the actions of the body, the body will disappear; if you watch your racing thoughts, the thought process, then the thoughts will disappear; and if you observe your emotions closely, then the emotions will disappear.

I have said that for the purification of emotions, allow love to come in place of hatred and friendship in place of enmity. Now I tell you to also be aware of this truth: there is a dimension behind the one who is loving and the one who is hating, which is just awareness – which neither loves nor hates. It is simply a witness. It sometimes watches hatred and sometimes watches love happening, but it is simply a witnessing, it is simply a watching.

When I hate someone, don't I at some point become aware of the fact that I am hating? And when I love someone, don't I somehow know inside that I am loving someone? That which is aware is behind the love and the hatred. It is your consciousness which is behind your body, thoughts and emotions – behind everything. This is why the old scriptures call it *neti-neti*, neither this nor that. It is neither the body nor the thoughts nor the emotions. It is none of these. And where there is nothing, there is the watcher, the seer, the witnessing consciousness, the soul.

So remember to be a watcher of your emotions also. Eventually you will have to come to that which is only pure seeing. That which is pure seeing has to be saved. That pure seeing is intelligence. We have called that pure seeing wisdom. We call that pure seeing consciousness. That is the ultimate goal of yoga and all the religions.

The basic quality of inner spiritual discipline is right-observation, right-observation of the actions of the body, of the thought process and of the inner currents of emotions. A person who becomes a witness after having passed through these three layers will reach the other shore. And to reach the other shore is to almost reach the goal. Someone who remains caught up in any of these three is still tied to this shore. He has not yet reached the goal.

I have heard a story:

It was a full-moon night...like tonight. The moon was full and it was a very beautiful night, so some friends felt like going boating in the middle of the night. They wanted to have some fun, so before climbing into the boat they had a lot to drink. Then they got into the boat, took the oars and started to row the boat. They rowed for a long time.

When the morning was breaking and a cold wind began to blow, they regained their senses and thought, "How far have we come? We have been rowing all night."

But when they looked closely they saw that they were still alongside the same bank where they had been the night before. Then they realized what they had forgotten to do: they had rowed the boat for such a long time, but they had forgotten to untie it.

And however much someone who has not untied his boat from the bank may suffer and cry, in this infinite ocean of the divine, he will not get anywhere.

To what is your boat of consciousness tied? – it is tied to your body, to your thoughts and to your emotions. The body, the thoughts and the emotions – that is your shore. In a drunken state you can go on rowing for lifetimes, for endless lifetimes. And after endless lifetimes when the cool breeze of awakened thinking, of some wisdom touches you, when some ray of light touches you and you wake up and look, you will find that you have wasted lifetimes rowing your boat and that you have been tethered to the same shore where you started. And then you will see the simple fact that you have forgotten to untie the boat.

Learn how to untie the boat. To row is very easy, but to untie the boat is very difficult. Ordinarily it is very easy to untie the boat and to row it is more difficult. But where the stream of life is concerned, it is very difficult to untie the boat but to row is very easy. Ramakrishna once said, "Untie your boat, open your sails and the winds of the divine will take you – you will not even need to row."

What he said was true – if you untie the boat you will see that the winds of the divine are already blowing and they will take you to faraway shores. And unless you reach the further shores you will not know what bliss is. But first you have to untie your boat.

Meditation means that you untie the boat. Why were those people unable to untie their boat? They were drunk, they were unconscious. And in the morning when they felt the cold winds and came back to their senses, they found that the boat was still tied to the riverbank.

I have spoken of right-watchfulness. Right-watching is the opposite of unconsciousness. You are in an unconscious state, and this is why you have tied the boat to your body, to your thoughts and to your emotions. If by feeling the cold winds of right-observation you become alert, then it will not be difficult to untie the boat. Unconsciousness is holding on to the boat, consciousness will set the boat free. And right-observation in all actions is the way to consciousness.

There is only one inner spiritual discipline and that is right-remembrance – right-remembrance or right-intelligence or right-consciousness. Remember this, because it is very important to use it constantly, continuously.

If the three purifications and the three emptinesses can happen…. The three purifications will help to bring the three emptinesses. If the three emptinesses are experienced it is *samadhi*, enlightenment. Samadhi is the door to truth, to the self, to the divine. For the one who awakens in samadhi, the world disappears. To disappear does not mean that these walls will disappear and that you will disappear. To disappear means that these walls will no longer be walls and you will no longer be you. When a leaf moves, you will not only see the leaf but also the lifeforce which moves it; and when the winds blow you will not only feel the winds but also the powers which make them blow; and then even in each and every particle of dirt you will see not only the mortal, but also the immortal. The world will disappear in the sense that the divine will have appeared.

God is not the creator of the world. Today somebody was asking me, "Who created the world?"

You are near the mountains, you are in the valleys and you are asking, "Who created these valleys and these trees? Who created them?" You will go on asking this until you experience for yourself. And once you have come to know you will no longer ask who created them, you will know – it is existence itself. There is no creator. Existence itself is the creator. When you have eyes you will be able to see, you will see that the creation itself is the creator. And this vast world around you will become the divine. The divine is not experienced in opposition to the world: when the worldly attitude disappears, the divine appears.

In that state of samadhi you will know the truth – that veiled truth, the truth which is normally hidden. And what is it hidden by? It is hidden only by your unawareness. There are no veils covering truth, the veils are over your own eyes. This is why one who drops the veils from his eyes comes to know truth.

And I have told you how to remove the veils from in front of your eyes – the three purifications and the three emptinesses will help you to remove these veils from your eyes.

And when the eyes are without any veils, it is called samadhi. That pure vision without any veils is samadhi.

Samadhi is the ultimate goal of religion – of all religions, of all the yogas. I have talked about it. Reflect on it, contemplate on it and meditate on it. Think about it, give it some thought and let it sink into your being. Just like a gardener, someone who sows seeds will one day find that flowers have blossomed. And someone who works hard digging in the mines will one day find diamonds and precious stones. And someone who dives into the water and goes deep will one day find he has brought up pearls.

One who has the longing and who is courageous will find his life transformed, he will make progress. To climb a mountain is not as great a challenge as to know oneself. And it is humiliation for an intelligent person who has the strength and energy to not know himself. Every single person can have the determination to know the truth, to know himself and to know enlightenment. With this resolve and by using these foundations it is possible for *anyone* to succeed. Think about this.

Now we will sit for the night meditation. Again, I will tell you something about the night meditation. Yesterday I told you about the five chakras in the body: there are parts of your body connected to these chakras. If you relax those chakras, if you go on suggesting to them that they are relaxing, then those particular parts of your body will simultaneously become relaxed.

The first chakra is the m*uladhar* chakra. The first chakra can be felt near the genitals. You will instruct this chakra to become relaxed. Focus your attention on it totally, tell it to become relaxed.

You will think, "But what is going to happen just by saying it? How will my legs become relaxed just because I tell them to relax? If I tell the body to freeze, how will it freeze?"

It does not take much intelligence to understand such a small thing. When you say to yourself, "Hand, pick up the handkerchief!" – how does the hand pick up the handkerchief? And when you tell your feet to walk, how do they walk? And when you tell your feet not to walk, how do they stop? Each and every atom of your body follows your orders. If it did not follow your orders, the body could not function. You tell the eyes to close and they close. There is a thought within, and the eyes close. Why? Do you think there is no connection between the thought and the eyes? If there were not you could sit inside thinking that your eyes should close, and they might not close. And you could be thinking that your feet should walk, and they might not move.

Whatever the mind says, it simultaneously reaches the body. If you are just a little intelligent you can make your body do anything. What you are making it do every day is just natural. But do you know that even that is not absolutely natural; even there, the power of suggestion is working. Do you know that if a human child is brought up among animals, he will not be able to stand upright? Incidents like this have happened.

Some time ago, in the forests near Lucknow, there was such an incident. A boy was found who had been brought up by wolves. Wolves like to carry children off from the village, and sometimes the wolves have also reared them. Many such

202

incidents have taken place. So about four years ago a fourteen-year-old boy who had been reared by the wolves was taken from the forest. The wolves had carried him off from the village as a small child, and they had fed him milk and reared him.

That fourteen-year-old boy was absolutely a wolf: he walked on all fours, he could not stand upright. He made wolf-like sounds, and he was ferocious, dangerous. If he had got hold of a human being he would have eaten him alive, but he was not able to speak. Now why would a boy of fourteen not be able to speak? And if you told him to speak, to try to speak, what would he do? And why would a fourteen-year-old boy not stand upright? – because it was never suggested to him to stand upright, so it never occurred to him to do it.

When a small child is born in your house, when he sees all of you walking it gives him the idea. Seeing people walking all around him, his courage grows and slowly, slowly he gets the idea that it is possible to stand up on two feet and to walk. He gets the idea, and it penetrates deeper into his consciousness. Then he gets the courage to walk and makes the effort. When he sees others speaking, he gets the idea that it is possible to speak; then he makes the effort to speak. The vocal chords which enable him to speak become activated.

There are many glands within us which are not active. Remember, the total development of man has not yet happened. Those who know the science of the body say that only a very small part of man's brain is active. The remaining part is totally inactive, it does not appear to have any function. And scientists have not been able to discover their function. As yet, those parts appear to have no function. A large part of your brain is lying there totally unused. But yoga says that all these parts can become active. And descending from the human beings, in animals an even smaller part is used – the greater part of an animal's brain is unused. When you descend the ladder even further, an even greater part of the brain of the lower animals is unused.

If we had been able to examine the brains of Buddha and Mahavira, we would have found that their entire brain was used; no part was dormant. Their whole brain capacity was used, and in you only a small part is used.

Now in order for that part which is not used to become active, you will have to give yourself suggestions; you will have to make an effort. Yoga has tried to make those parts of the brain active by working on the chakras. Yoga is a science, and a time will come when yoga will become the greatest science in the world.

As I have said, by focusing your attention on these five chakras and by making suggestions to those particular parts of your body, these chakras will become instantly relaxed. You will give the first chakra a suggestion to relax and simultaneously you will imagine that the feet are relaxing – and the feet *will* become relaxed. Then you will move upwards. You will suggest to the second chakra near the navel to become relaxed, and all the organs around the navel will relax. Then you will move upwards, and you will suggest to the third chakra near the heart that it should relax, and the whole complex of the heart will become relaxed. And again move upwards and suggest to the fourth chakra between the eyes that it should become relaxed, and all the muscles of your face will relax. Move upwards even further and suggest to the fifth chakra that it should relax, and everything inside the brain will become relaxed and silent.

The more total you are in making the suggestions, the more total the happening will be. After practicing it continually for a few days you will start to feel the results.

Don't be afraid if you don't feel results right away. If nothing happens quickly, there is no need to feel anxious. Even if it takes many lives for someone who is thirsty to discover the soul, it is not much time. It takes us years just to learn ordinary things. So by doing this experiment with total determination, patience and silence, the results are assured.

You will relax the body by giving suggestions to these five chakras. Then, when I tell you to relax the breathing, let it relax. And I will tell you that your breathing is becoming silent…then make the suggestion. Finally I will tell you that your thoughts are disappearing and the mind is becoming empty.

This will be our meditation experiment. But before this meditation, we will make these suggestions for two minutes, and before making these suggestions for two minutes we will make the resolution five times.

Now we will start the night meditation. Everybody has to lie down for this meditation. It is only to be done lying down. So make space for yourself. We will sit and make the resolution, make the suggestions, and then lie down.

THE PATH OF MEDITATION

truth: your birthright

Chapter 8

My Beloved Ones,

*S*OMEONE has asked: *What is truth? Is it possible to know it partially? And if not, then what can one do to attain it? Because it is not possible for every person to be a sage.*

First, each person has the potential to become a sage. It is a different matter if someone does not transform this potential into a reality. It is a different matter if a seed is unable to grow into a tree, but every seed has the intrinsic capacity for becoming a tree. Every seed has this potential. That it does not become one is an entirely different matter. If it does not get fertilized, does not find any soil, does not get any water or light, the seed will die, that is possible, but the seed did have the potential.

Each and every person has the potential to become a sage. That is why you should first of all drop this idea from your mind that to become enlightened is the special privilege of only some people. To become enlightened is not the right of any special people. And the people who have spread this idea are only doing it to feed their egos. If someone says that it is very difficult to become enlightened and possible for only very few people, it nourishes their ego. This is just a way for some people to fulfill their ego. Otherwise, everyone has the potential to be a sage, because there is space and opportunity for everyone to experience truth.

I said it is another thing if you don't experience it. For that, only you will be responsible, your potential will not be responsible. All of us sitting here have the power to get up and walk, but if we don't walk and go on sitting, then what? You discover your powers by making them active; you don't know them until you use them.

Right now you are just sitting here, and no one can know that you have the capacity to walk. And if you look inside yourself, even you will not be able to locate this capacity to walk. You will not be able to find it. You will only know whether you have the capacity to walk after you try to walk. And only after you go through the process of trying to become enlightened will you know if you have the potential or not. Those who don't try will definitely feel that only some people have this potential. This is wrong.

So the first thing: you have to understand that to attain to truth is everyone's right, it is everyone's birthright. In this respect no one has any special rights.

And the second thing which has been asked is: "What is truth? And is it possible to know it partially?"

Truth cannot be known partially, because truth is one. It cannot be broken into parts. This means that it is not possible for a person to know a little bit of truth now, then a little bit more, and then a little bit more. It does not happen like this. Truth is experienced as one. This means that it is not a gradual process. It is experienced totally, it is experienced in an explosion. But if I say that it can only be known totally, you will feel a little apprehensive because you feel so weak, how can you possibly know it totally?

When a man climbs up to the roof of the house he reaches it all at once, yet he has climbed the steps to it one at a time. He does not reach the roof in one step. When he is on the first step he is not on the roof and when he is on the last step he is still not on the roof; he begins to approach the roof, but he is still not on it.

It is possible to move closer to the truth gradually, but when you arrive at truth it is total. This means that you can gradually move closer to truth, but the attainment of truth is total, it is never in parts. It is never in fragments, remember this.

So the introduction to meditation that I have given you is a set of steps: you will not know truth through them, but you will move closer to truth through them. And at the last step which I have called 'emptiness of the emotions', when you jump beyond this emptiness of the emotions too, you experience truth. But then truth is known in its totality.

The experience of the divine does not come in fragments, it happens as a whole. But the way to reach the divine is divided into many parts. Remember this: the way to reach the divine is divided into parts, but truth itself is not in parts. So don't think, "How can a person as weak as I am know the whole truth? I can only manage to know it if it can be known bit by bit."

No, you will also be able to know it because you only need to walk on the path for a short distance at a time. It is not possible to walk the whole length of the path all at once. You cannot walk the whole length of a path at once; you have to walk a little at a time. But the destination is always reached as a whole, you never get there in parts – remember this.

Someone has asked: *What is truth?*

There is no way to say it in words. To this day, it has been impossible to say it in human language – and it will never be said in the future either. It is not that in the past we did not have a language rich enough to say it, and that we will be able to say it in the future. It will never be said.

There is a reason for this. Languages developed for the purpose of communicating with other people. Language was created in order to communicate with people, it was not created to express truth. And it is unlikely that any of the people who created language had known truth. This is why there is no word for the ultimate truth. And the people who knew truth did not know it through language, they knew it through silence. This means that when they experienced truth they were totally silent, no word existed there. So there is a problem: when they started talking about it after the experience, they found one point, truth, which there was no way to describe. It is not possible to provide words for it. And when they provided words, the words were incomplete, they fell short.

And on the basis of these words alone, conflicts arose – based on these very same words! Because all words are inadequate, they are unable to express truth. They are just like hints. It is as if somebody is pointing his finger to the moon, and if we grab his finger thinking that this is the moon, then there will be trouble. The finger is not the moon. The finger is just an indication. Whoever grabs hold of the indication will be in trouble. You have to let go of the finger so that the thing to which it is pointing becomes visible. You have to drop the words, and only then will you have a glimpse of truth. But someone who grabs hold of the words will miss the experience.

This is why there is no way for me to tell you what truth is. And if somebody claims to be telling you, he is deceiving himself. If somebody tells you this, he is deceiving himself and you. There is no way to describe truth. Yes, there is a way to tell you how to experience truth. The method to know truth, the process, can be described, but what truth is cannot be said.

There are methods to attain truth, but there are no definitions of truth. During these three days I have discussed these methods, and you may feel that we have completely ignored truth itself. I have talked about truth, but I have never said what truth actually is.

No, it cannot be said, it can only be experienced. Truth cannot be described but it can be experienced – and it will be *your* experience. The method can be given, but the experience of truth will be your own. The experience of truth is always individual, and it is not possible to communicate it to another.

So this is why I will not tell you what truth is. It is not because I want to withhold something from you, but because it cannot be said. In ages past, during the time of the Upanishads, whenever it happened that someone would go to a sage and ask, "What is truth?" the sage would look hard at the person.

Again the person would ask, "What is truth?" Then he would ask a third time, "What is truth?"

And the sage would say, "I tell you again and again, but you don't understand."

The person would say, "What are you saying? I have asked

you three times, and all three times you were silent. And you say that you have told me again and again?"

Then the sage would say, "I wish you were able to understand my silence, because then you will have understood what truth is."

Silence is the only way to say it. Those who have known truth have become silent. When truth is talked about, they become silent.

If you can be silent, you can know it. If you are not silent you will not be able to know it. You can know the truth, but you cannot make another person know it. This is why I won't say what truth is – because it cannot be said.

Someone has asked: *Are a person's actions bound by the result of the actions of many lives, and if so, then what is left in the hands of the individual in this life?*

The question is: "If we are controlled by our actions in the past and the values of our past lives, what can we do now?" It has been rightly asked. If it is true that a person is absolutely bound by his past actions, then what is in his own hands? What can he do in the present? And if it is true that he is not at all bound by his actions of the past, then what is the point in doing anything? – because if he is not bound by his past actions, he will not be bound tomorrow by whatever he does now. So if he does something good today there will be no possibility to benefit from that good deed tomorrow. And if he is totally bound by his actions in the past there will be no meaning in anything he does – because he cannot do anything, he will be totally bound.

On the other hand, if he is totally free there will be no point in doing anything, because whatever he does tomorrow he will be free of it, and his past actions will not affect him. That is why man is neither completely bound nor completely free: one of his legs is tied and the other is free.

Once somebody asked Hazrat Ali, "Is man free or bound by his actions?"

Ali said, "Raise one of your legs."

The man was free to raise either his left or right leg. He raised his left leg. Then Ali said, "Now raise the other one."

And the man replied, "Are you mad? I cannot raise the other one now."

Ali asked, "Why?"

The man answered, "I can only raise one at a time."

Ali said, "The same is the case with man's life. You always have two legs but you are able to raise only one at a time; one is always tied." This is why the possibility exists for you to free the leg which is bound with the help of the leg which is free to move. But the possibility also exists for you to tie the one which is free with the help of the one which is tied up.

Whatsoever you have done in the past, you have done. You were free to do it, you have done it. Part of you has become frozen and is bound, but another part of you is still free. You are free to do the opposite of what you did. You can cancel what you did before by doing the opposite. You can destroy it by doing something different. You can dismiss it by doing something better. It is in the hands of the individual to wash away all his past conditionings.

Until yesterday you were angry; you were free to be angry. Certainly, someone who has been angry every day for the last twenty years will be bound by anger. For example, there are two people: the one who has been continuously angry for twenty years gets up in the morning one day and cannot find his slippers next to his bed; the one who has not been angry in twenty years also gets up in the morning and does not find his slippers next to his bed – which of them is more likely to get angry in this situation? Anger will arise in the first man, the man who has been angry for twenty years.

In this sense he is tied, because the twenty-year-old habit of becoming angry will immediately arise in him when something does not happen the way he wants it to happen. He is tied in the sense that twenty years of conditioning will make him feel inclined to do the same thing he has always done. But is he so tied that there is no possibility for him not to become angry?

No, nobody is ever that bound. If he can become aware right this moment, then he can stop. It is possible not to allow the anger to come. It is possible to transform the anger. And if he does that, the habit of twenty years may prove to be a problem but it will not be able to stop him completely – because if the one who has created the habit moves against it, he then has the freedom to completely destroy it. Just by experimenting with it a dozen times he can be free of it.

Past actions bind you, but they don't bind you completely. Actions grip you, but they don't grip you completely. They have their chains, but all chains can be broken; there is no chain which will not break. And something which does not break cannot be called a chain.

Chains bind you, but intrinsic to all chains is the possibility that they can be broken. If there is a chain which cannot be broken, you will not be able to call it a chain. Only what binds you but can also be broken can be called a chain.

Your actions are chains in the sense that those chains can also be broken. One's consciousness is always free. You are always free to go back over the steps that you have taken and the path that you have walked on.

So the past is restricting you, but your future is totally free. One leg is bound and the other is free. The leg of the past is tied, the leg of the future is free. If you want to, you can raise this leg of the future in the same direction as where the leg of the past is tied. Then you will go on being tied up. If you want to you can raise the leg of the future in the direction that is opposite to the leg of the past – and you will go on becoming free, it is in your hands. The state when both legs are free is called *moksha*, enlightenment. And the absolutely lowest kind of hell is the state where both legs are bound.

For this reason there is no need to be afraid of the past, or of past lives, because one who has done those actions is still free to do other actions.

Someone has asked: *Who is it that thinks after becoming a witness?*

When you are a witness there is no thought. The moment you think something, you are no longer a witness. I am standing in the garden and I become a witness to a flower, I am looking at the flower – if I am only looking I am a witness, and if I start thinking then I am not a witness. The moment I start to think, the flower will no longer be there before my eyes – the current of thought will come between me and the flower. When I look at the flower and say, "The flower is beautiful," the moment my mind says that the

216

flower is beautiful I am not seeing the flower. Because the mind does not do two things at the same time – a thin curtain comes in between. And if I start thinking, "I have seen this flower before, this flower is familiar," this flower has disappeared from my eyes. Now I am just imagining that I am seeing it.

Once I took a friend who had come from far away boating on the river. He had just come back from far away countries. He had seen many rivers and many lakes, and he was full of thoughts about those rivers and lakes. When I took him boating on a full-moon night, he kept on talking about lakes in Switzerland and about lakes in Kashmir. After an hour, when we were returning, he said to me, "The place where you took me was really beautiful."

I said, "You are lying. You didn't even see the place. I felt the whole time that you might just as well have been in Switzerland or in Kashmir, but you were not present in the boat we were sitting in.

"And now I also want to tell you this," I said to him, "When you were in Switzerland you must have been some-where else. And when you were in Kashmir you cannot have been on the lake about which you were talking. Not only am I saying that you did not see the lake to which I took you – I am telling you that you have not seen any of these lakes."

The curtain of your thoughts does not allow you to be a witness. Your thoughts don't allow you to be a witness. But when you drop thoughts, when you become separate from your thoughts, then you become a witness. The absence of thoughts makes you a witness. But while I am telling you to become a witness, you are asking, "Who is thinking?"

No, there is no one who is thinking, there is only the

witness, and that witness is your interiority. If you are in a state of total witnessing – where no thought arises, where no wave of thoughts arises – then you will enter into yourself. In the same way, when there is no wave in the ocean, no movement, then its surface becomes silent and you are able to see below the surface.

Thought is a wave, thought is a disease and thought is excitement. You attain to witnessing when you have lost the excitement of thought. When you are witnessing, no one is thinking. If you think, you are no longer witnessing. Thinking and witnessing is a contradiction.

This is why we have made such a total effort to understand this method of meditation. In fact, we have been doing experiments in dropping thought. And in the experiment that we are doing here, you are making thoughts very weak so that you come to the state where there are no thoughts and only the thinker is there. By the thinker I mean the one who thinks – only he is present, but he is not thinking. And when he does not think then seeing happens. Try to understand this: thinking and witnessing are two opposite things. That is why I said before that only blind people think. Those who have eyes don't think. If I don't have eyes and I want to leave this house, I will think, "Where is the door?" If I don't have eyes and I want to get out of this building, I will think, "Where is the door?" But if I have eyes, what is there to think about? I will see the way out and leave. So the point is that if I have eyes I will see the way out, why would I think about it?

The less people can see, the more they think. The world calls them thinkers, but I say they are blind. And the more people can see, the less they think.

Mahavira and Buddha were not great thinkers. I hear very intelligent people say that they were great thinkers. That is absolutely wrong. They were not thinkers at all because they were not blind. In India we call them seers, watchers.

This is why in India we call the science of this method *darshan*, seeing. Darshan means to see. We don't call it philosophy; philosophy and darshan are not synonymous. Often people call darshan 'philosophy', but this is wrong. It is wrong to call the darshan of India, Indian philosophy; it is not a philosophy at all. Philosophy means thinking, contemplating, reflecting. And darshan means to drop all thinking, contemplating and reflecting.

There have been thinkers in the West, the West has its philosophy. They have thought about what truth is – they have *thought* about it. In India we don't think about what truth is, we think about how we can experience the truth. That is, we think about how to open the eyes. This is why our whole process is one of opening the eyes. Our whole work is to open the eyes.

Logic develops only where there is thought. The connection, the relationship of thoughts is through logic. And the connection, the relationship of darshan, seeing, is through yoga.

No logic has developed in the East. We have not loved logic at all. We have considered it to be a game, a children's game. We have looked for something else – we have looked for darshan, seeing, and to attain that we have looked towards yoga. Yoga is a process by which you can open your eyes and see. And to see, experiment with being a witness. Thoughts will become weaker and a moment will come when there is no-thought. I am not talking about

219

a lack of thoughts, but no-thought.

There is a big difference between a lack of thoughts and no-thought. Someone who is in a state where thoughts are lacking is below the thinker, and someone who is in a state of no-thought is much higher than the thinker. A state where there are no currents of thoughts in the mind is the state of no-thought: the mind is silent and the ability to witness arises out of that silence. The state where there is a lack of thoughts is one where one does not understand what to do.

So I am telling you to come to a state of no-thought, not to a lack of thought. The person who lacks thoughts is someone who does not understand. A person in a state of no-thought is someone who not only understands, but is also able to witness. And the witness will take you towards knowing, towards your inner soul.

The experiments that we have done to awaken the witnessing of the breath, or of meditation, are simply to enable you to experience the moment when *you* are present but there are no thoughts. If you can experience that pure moment when you are there but there are no thoughts, even for a moment, then you will have found a very rare treasure in your life.

Move in that direction and make an effort to achieve it, and make the moment when there will be consciousness but no thoughts your greatest longing.

When consciousness is empty of thoughts you experience truth. And when consciousness is full of thoughts, when consciousness is repressed, then you don't experience truth. Just as when the sky is covered with clouds the sun is not visible, in the same way, when the mind is covered with thoughts your inner kingdom is not visible. If you want to see the sun you will have to disperse the clouds and get rid of them so that the sun can shine out from behind them. You will also need to get rid of thoughts in the same way, so that the inner kingdom can be felt and experienced.

This morning when I was coming out of the house somebody asked me, "Is enlightenment possible in this age?"

I said to him, "Yes, it is possible."

The question that he then asked me was, "If enlightenment is possible in this age, then can you tell what the question is that I want to ask you?"

If you think the meaning of enlightenment is to have just the capacity to tell what your next question is going to be, then you are making a big mistake. You will be fooled by a snake-charmer, you will be fooled by a juggler performing on the streets for a few *paisa*. For a few paisa this juggler can tell you what is in your mind. And if ever an enlightened person were to agree to this idea, he would not be an enlightened person.

The meaning of enlightenment is not that you are able to tell what is going through someone's mind. You have just not understood its meaning. Enlightenment means the state of consciousness where there is nothing to be known, where there is no one to know and only pure knowing remains. The meaning of enlightenment is that only pure knowing remains.

Right now, whenever you know something there are three things involved: first there is the knower – he is the one who knows; then there is what he knows – the object; and then there is the relationship between these two – which is the knowing. This state of pure knowing, enlightenment, remains suppressed by the knower and the object.

221

Enlightenment means that the object has disappeared. And when the object disappears how can there be a knower? When the object disappears, the knower also disappears. Then what will be left behind? Then only pure knowing will be left behind. In that moment of knowing, you realize ultimate liberation. So enlightenment means to experience pure knowing. What I have called enlightenment is the experience of pure knowing. This is the truth which all the different religions have talked about. Hence, different religions have different words for truth. What Patanjali has called *samadhi*, Jainas have called *keval gyan*, ultimate knowing, and Buddha has called *pragya*.

Enlightenment does not mean that you can tell what is going through someone else's head. That is a very easy thing. That is just ordinary telepathy, thought-reading; it has nothing to do with enlightenment. And if you are really curious to know what is going on in someone else's head, I can tell you how to find out what is going on in the mind of the person sitting next to you. I will not tell you what is going on in *your* mind, but I can tell you how to know what is going on in other people's minds – that will be easier.

In the meditation experiment you make the resolution that I have been speaking about, where you exhale all your breath and wait for a moment without breathing – in the same way when you go home, try this experiment with a small child for three or four days, and you will understand what I mean: exhale completely and have the child sit in front of you, and when there is no breath left inside you, then with absolute determination, with your eyes closed, try to see what is going through the child's mind. And tell the child to think about something small...the name of a flower.

Don't tell the child which one, but ask him to think of the name of a flower on his own. Then, closing your eyes and throwing your breath out, strengthen the determination to see what is going through his mind.

In two to three days you will be able to see it. And even if you are able to see only one word it does not matter, because then you can also see sentences. It is a long process.

But don't think that this means you have attained to ultimate knowing! It has nothing to do with ultimate knowing. It is knowledge about the mind when you are able to read what is going on in another person's mind. And for this there is no need to be religious, and there is no need to be a saint.

There is much work being done on this in the West. There are many psychic societies which are working on telepathy and thought-reading, and they have developed a scientific system. Within a century or even half a century every doctor will be able to use it, every teacher will be able to use it. Every shopkeeper will use it to know his customers' preferences, and it will all be used to exploit people. This has nothing whatsoever to do with ultimate knowing, it is simply a technique. But the technique is not known to many people, and this is why you think of it as something extraordinary. If you experiment a little you will be surprised, and you may even be able to understand something. But this is not enlightenment. Enlightenment is a very different matter.

Enlightenment means to experience the ultimate state of pure knowing. In that state you experience the immortal, and what I have called *satchitanand*, truth-consciousness-bliss.

One friend has asked: *Is it possible to glimpse the ultimate without enlightenment?*

No, it is not possible. Enlightenment is only a door. It is as if somebody were to ask whether it is possible to enter this house without a door. Then what would you say? You would say that it is not possible. And even if he got in by breaking a wall, you would still call that hole in the wall an entrance, you would call it a door. But it is not possible to enter a house without a door. However you enter, it will have to be through a door. If you are intelligent you will enter through the door, if you are unintelligent you will break a hole in a wall somewhere.

Except enlightenment, there is no way. Enlightenment is the door to the ultimate, to truth. And without a door, I don't see how you can enter – no one has ever entered without a door.

Remember this, and don't think that the ultimate will be possible without samadhi. The mind is like this: it hopes there might be a cheaper way. It suggests that there is a path that you don't have to walk for yourself. But you have to walk on your path. That is what a path means, that you create it by walking on it. You want there to be a door that you don't have to pass through and yet still reach the destination. But there is no door that will lead you somewhere unless you pass through it.

But the mind has many weaknesses. One of the weaknesses of the mind is that you want to get something for nothing. Especially when it comes to experiencing the ultimate, you have the idea that it is only worth considering if you can get it without doing anything for it. And, in actual fact, even if someone were ready to give it to you for nothing, you would think twice about whether to accept it or not.

Once there was a *sadhu,* a monk in Sri Lanka, and every day he would talk about enlightenment, about nirvana, about samadhi. Some people had been listening to him for years.

One day a man stood up and said to him, "I want to ask you, so many people have been listening to you for such a long time – has anyone become enlightened?"

The monk said, "If that's what you are asking, let's make you enlightened today. Are you ready? If you are ready, then it is my truth that I will make you enlightened today."

But the man said, "Today? Let me think about it a little. Someday…. Just like that, today? Let me think about it a little. I will come again and tell you."

If somebody were to tell you that he could introduce you to God right this minute, I don't think your mind would immediately say yes. Your mind would start thinking about it. I am talking to you about truth, and your mind will start thinking whether or not to know it. Even if you could get God for free, you would think about it first. When you are paying a price for something it is quite natural to think about it – but the mind always wants everything for free. Whatever seems to have no value to your mind you want for free. Whatever seems to have a value to your mind you will pay a price for.

If you care even a little about experiencing the divine, you will feel that you are ready to give up everything for it. If you have to give up everything for just a glimpse of the divine, you will be ready to do it.

Someone has asked, "Is it possible to glimpse the ultimate without enlightenment?" No, it is not possible. It is not possible without effort. It is not possible without resolve. It is not possible without your total commitment and devotion.

But this kind of weak people give the cunning people an opportunity to exploit them. A kind of religious exploitation goes on all over the world, because you want to get something for nothing. Some people will tell you that you can get what you want with their blessings: "Worship me, fall at my feet, remember my name, have faith in me and you will achieve it all." And because people are weak they believe this, and they waste their lives touching their feet. You will not gain anything this way, it is just exploitation.

No guru can give you enlightenment. He can show you the path how to reach it, but you will have to walk on the path yourself. No guru can walk for you; no one in this world can walk for someone else. Your own legs make you walk, and you have to walk on your own legs. And if someone says – and there are many who say – "We want only one thing from you: that you have faith in us and we will do the rest"...they are exploiting you. And because you are weak you allow them to exploit you.

All the religious hypocrisy that is happening in the world is happening more because of your weakness than because of the hypocrites. If you were not weak no religious hypocrisy in the world would stand a chance. If a man has even a little strength and courage, if he feels even a little pride and respect for his life and somebody says to him, "I will make you attain the divine through my blessings," he will say, "Forgive me, but this would be a great insult." In fact, he would say, "Can there be anything more insulting to me than the idea that I should attain the ultimate through *your* blessings?"

And what is given by somebody as a favour can also be taken away just as easily. What have you gained when what has been given as a favor can be taken away with the loss of this favor? And an enlightenment that can be given and taken away, an enlightenment that can be given to you by somebody else, would simply be a deception.

No one in this world can give truth and enlightenment to anyone else. You will have to experience it through your own effort and devotion. So don't think this even for a moment, because your weakness will prove fatal to you. And not only will it destroy you, it will also make it possible for the hypocrites, the deceivers and the false gurus to multiply. They are false, they have no value, and what's more they are dangerous and destructive.

Someone has asked: *What should the energy of the ego be changed into?*

I have told you that if the energy of anger arises you can transform it creatively. I have also told you that if it is sex energy, that too can be transformed. The ego is not an energy in the same way that anger, sex and greed are energies. The ego is not an energy in that sense. Anger sometimes arises, the urge for sex is there only sometimes, greed also only grips your consciousness sometimes. The ego does not only exist sometimes: until you are enlightened it is always with you. It is not an energy, it is your state. Try to understand the difference.

The ego is not an energy, it is your state of being. It does not come and go; it is always with you, it is standing behind all your actions. It is your state. Many things come because of it but the ego itself is always there. Anger arises because of ego. If you are an egoist you will be more angry. If you are an egoist you will be more greedy for fame, more greedy, and hungry for power. If you are an egoist, these things will arise in you because of ego. Ego is the state of your consciousness; and as long as there is ignorance, there is ego. But when knowing arises ego disappears, and in its place you experience your being.

Ego is an invisible covering surrounding your being. Ego is a curtain around being. It is not energy, it is ignorance. Many energies arise because of this ignorance, and if you use them in a destructive way, the ego-state goes on becoming stronger. But if you use these arising energies in a creative way, the strength of the ego will go on weakening, the ego-state will become weaker. If all your energies are used in a creative way, the ego will one day disappear. And when the smoke of the ego disappears, behind it you will come across the flame of your being. The smoke of the ego surrounds the flame of your soul. When the unconsciousness clears, when the smoke of the ego clears away, when all the layers of 'I' disappear, and when the idea that 'I am' has also disappeared, then you experience the depths.

Ramakrishna used to tell a story that once a statue made of salt went to see a fair at the seashore. And at the seashore he saw that the sea was infinite. On the way somebody asked, "How deep is it?"

And the statue said, "I will go and find out."

So he jumped into the water. Many days passed and many years passed, and yet the statue never returned. He had said, "I will go and find out" – but he was a statue made of salt. The moment he jumped into the ocean the salt dissolved and disappeared, and he never found the bottom of the ocean.

The 'I' that searches for godliness for the depths of the ocean disappears in the searching. It is just a statue made of salt, not an energy.

So when you embarked on your search for the divine, you started with the idea "I am going to find the divine." But as you go on searching you will find that the divine is nowhere to be found and the seeker also is disappearing. A moment comes when the 'I' becomes totally empty, and then you discover that you have found the divine.

This means that the 'I' will never meet the divine. When the 'I' is not there, only then is the divine there. But as long as the 'I' is there the divine will never be found. That is why Kabir has said, "The path of love is very narrow – there cannot be two on it."

There can be either you or the divine. And as long as you are there, there cannot be the divine. And when you disappear, godliness is.

This ego is the only ignorance. And many of your life-energies are misused because of this ignorance. If you use them rightly the ego will not get any nourishment, and slowly, slowly it will disappear.

So if you try what I have called the three experiments for the purification of life – the purification of the body, the purification of thoughts and the purification of emotions –if you go on doing these three experiments, one day you will find that the ego has disappeared. Anger will not disappear, ego will disappear. The energy of anger will be there in new forms, but the ego will not be there. When the ego disappears, no trace is left behind. Anger or sex don't disappear, they are transformed. They will be present in a different form. The energy of anger will stay, but it will take a different form.

It is possible that it will become compassion -- but the energy will be the same.

And when the energy of people who are very hot-tempered is transformed, they become filled with an equal amount of compassion because the energy takes a new form. The energy is not destroyed, it simply takes a new form.

I said earlier that the same people who are very sexual are the people who experience real celibacy, because the same sexual energy is transformed and becomes celibacy for them. But when the ego disappears it does not change into something else, because in the first place it was only ignorance. There is no question of its transformation: it was only an illusion. It is as if someone in the darkness thinks that a rope is a snake, but when he gets closer he sees that it is really a rope. Then if you ask him, "What became of the snake?" he will say, "Nothing became of the snake. There never was a snake." There is no question that it has changed into something else.

In the same way, the ego is the result of a misunderstanding about your being. It is a deluded perception of being. To think that the ego is the being is the same as thinking that a rope is a snake. As you reach closer to your being you will find that ego does not exist. So it will not transform into anything else – there is no question of a transformation because it simply doesn't exist! It was only an illusion which appeared to be there. Ego is ignorance, not energy – but if there is ignorance it causes you to misuse your energies. What happens in ignorance is the misuse of your energies.

So remember, there will be no change to the ego, there will be no transformation. The ego will simply disappear. It is not an energy in that sense.

And the last question: *Why is it necessary for the soul to become merged with existence?*

It would be better if you had asked, "What is the need for the soul to disappear into bliss?" It would have been better if you had asked, "What is the need for the soul to become healthy?" It would be better if you had asked, "What is the need for the soul to go from darkness into light?"

The only need for the soul to dissolve into the divine is that life can never be fulfilled through pain and suffering. In other words, suffering is always unacceptable to life. Life always desires bliss. And to suffer is to be separate from the divine. When you become one with the divine, life becomes bliss.

So it is not a question of God or of the divine, it is a question of your rising from suffering into bliss, of going from darkness to the light within you. But if you feel there is no need, then be satisfied with your suffering.

But nobody can be satisfied with being in misery. Misery, by its very nature, takes you away from yourself; bliss, by its very nature, pulls you back to yourself. The world is misery, the divine is bliss. The need to merge with the divine is not a religious need; the need to merge with the divine is a fundamental need.

So it can happen that someone will say no to God, but no one will say no to bliss. This is why I say that there is no such thing as an atheist. Only someone who rejects bliss can be an atheist. Everyone in this world is a theist – a theist in the sense that each person is thirsty for bliss.

There are two kinds of theists: one is a worldly theist, the other is a spiritual theist. One believes in the world, that he will find bliss through the world. The other believes that only in the spiritual realm will he know bliss. The people you call atheists are theists in their attitudes towards the world; their quest is also for bliss. They are also searching for bliss. And today or tomorrow, when they realize that there is no bliss in this world, there will be no other alternative for them but to become curious about the spiritual.

Your search is for bliss. No one's search is for the divine, your quest is for bliss. Bliss is godliness – I call the state of total bliss, godliness. The moment you are in a state of total bliss you are the divine. This means that the moment there is no desire left in you, you become the divine. Total bliss implies that no desire remains. If there is still some desire, there will still be some misery too. When there is no more any desire you are in total bliss – and only then are you one with existence.

You have asked, "What the need is to be one with the divine?" I will put it like this: there is a need to be one with the divine because you have needs. The day you have no needs, there will no longer be any need to be one with the divine – you will have become the divine.

Each person wants to be free of his needs. He longs for a moment of freedom where he is not bound by any needs, where he is just boundless and infinite; where there is nothing that remains to be attained. Nothing can be taken away and nothing can be left behind. That boundlessness and infiniteness is God.

God does not mean that there is a man sitting up there somewhere, and you will be able to see him and he will bless you, and you will sit at his feet and have fun in heaven. No such God exists anywhere. And if you are in search of such a

God, you are under an illusion. You will never find this God. Up to now, no one has ever been able to find this God.

God is the ultimate state of bliss of your consciousness. God is not a person but an experience. So you never come face to face with God in the sense that you meet him or you go to see him; a meeting in which he is standing in front of you and you are looking at him. Everything that you are looking at is imagination. When all imagination and all thoughts have disappeared from consciousness, suddenly you become aware that you are simply a living part of this infinite world, of this existence, of this universe. The pulsing of your heart becomes one with the pulse of the whole existence. Your breath becomes one with existence, your lifeforce starts beating as one with existence. No boundary remains, no difference between you and existence.

Then you know, "*Aham brahmasmi*, I am God." Then you realize that what you have known as your 'I' is an essential part of the whole of existence. "I am existence" – I call this the experience of godliness.

There are no more questions. Now, for a while, the people who are wanting to see me alone for a few minutes, can see me. If you want to ask something in private, you can do so.

THE PATH OF MEDITATION

one step at a time

Chapter 9

My Beloved Ones,

*D*URING THESE three days, great showers of love, peace and bliss have happened in your hearts. I am one of those birds who has no nest, but you have given me a place in your hearts – you have loved my thoughts and the outpourings of my heart. You have listened to them silently, and you have tried to understand them, and you have expressed love for them. I am grateful to you for that. I am grateful to you for what I have seen in your eyes, in your joy, in the tears that have come out of your joy.

I feel so happy. I am happy about the fact that I have been able to create a thirst for bliss in you. I feel happy that I have been able to make you feel discontented. This is what I see in my life, and perhaps this is my work – to make those who are quiet and satisfied discontented; to wake up the people who are moving along quietly and say to them that this life of theirs is not really life, that what they think of as life is just deception and death. Because a life which ends only in death cannot be considered to be life. Only a life which leads to the eternal life is truly life.

During these three days you have tried to live this true life, you have tried to focus on it. If your determination is strong, if your longing is deep, it will not be impossible to completely quench the thirst that you have quenched just a little during these days.

Tonight, at this moment of farewell, I will say a few more things to you. The first is that if the longing to experience the divine has become a flame within you, quickly put that longing into action. Someone who postpones to do something good will miss, and someone who hurries to do something bad will also miss. Someone who postpones doing good misses, and someone who hurries to do bad also misses.

This is one of life's keys: stop and postpone when you are about to do something bad, but don't stop and postpone when you are about to do something good.

If a good thought comes to your mind, it is helpful to start acting on it immediately because tomorrow is uncertain; the next moment is uncertain. Whether or not we will be, it is not possible to say. Before death takes us we have to prove conclusively that death alone was not meant to be our destiny. Before death, we have to learn how to experience something which is beyond death. And death can come at any time, it can come at any moment. I am talking now, and it can come this moment. So I need to be ready for it all the time; I have to be ready every moment. So don't postpone until tomorrow. If you feel something is right, act on it immediately..

Last night when we were sitting at the lake I told you about a lama in Tibet. Somebody had gone to see him and to ask him about truth. There was a tradition in Tibet that you circle around a lama three times, bow down at his feet and then ask your question. This young man went, but he did not circle around the lama or bow down at his feet. He just went to him and said, "I have a question! Give me an answer!"

The lama said, "First complete the formal rites."

The young man said, "You are demanding the ritual three rounds. I can walk around you three thousand times, but if I die during these three rounds before I have known truth, then whose responsibility will it be, mine or yours? So first answer my question and then I will complete the rounds." He said, "Who knows, I may die in the middle of the rounds."

So the most significant realization for the meditator is to be aware of the reality of death. He should be constantly aware that it can happen at any moment: "I will go to sleep tonight, and who knows...this may be my last night. I may never get up in the morning. So tonight I should go to bed in such a way that nothing is left incomplete and I can sleep peacefully. If death comes, it is welcome."

So don't postpone anything beautiful until tomorrow. And postpone anything bad as much as you can – death may come in between, and you will have been saved from doing something bad. If you get the idea to do something bad, postpone it for as long as you can. Death is not very far away – if you can just postpone some of your bad actions for ten or twenty years, your life could become divine. Death is not very far away, if someone is able to postpone his evil acts for a few years, his life can become pure. Death is not far away – and someone who postpones to do something good for too long will not experience any bliss in life.

So I want to remind you that there is an urgency to do something good. And if you are feeling something good, then just begin with that. Don't think and postpone it until tomorrow. A person who thinks about doing something tomorrow does not really want to do it. "I'll do it tomorrow" is a way of postponing. If you don't want to do something, you should be clear that you don't want to do it; that is another matter.

But to postpone until tomorrow is dangerous. The person who postpones something until tomorrow has in a way postponed it forever. Someone who leaves something until tomorrow has in a way dropped it forever.

If something in life feels right, then the moment it feels right is also the moment to act on it. You have to begin right in that moment.

So keep in mind the urgency of doing things that are good and of delaying things that are wrong. Also keep in mind that the keys that I have given you to experiment with about goodness and truth are not intellectual doctrines. In other words, I am not interested in explaining doctrines to you. I am not interested in academics. I have told you about these keys to persuade you to act on them. And if you act on them they can do something for you. If you are ready to act on them, these keys will help you. And if you use them, they will transform you. These keys are very alive, they are like fire: if you kindle them even a little, you can experience the birth of the new man in you.

The first birth we get from our parents. It is not a birth, it is only the arrival of one more new death. It is another cycle that will end in death. It is not a birth, it is only taking on a new body.

There is another birth which you don't get through your parents, but which happens through meditation. And that is the real birth. It is only after this birth that one becomes a *dwija*, twice-born. One has to give this birth to oneself. So don't feel satisfied and at rest until you have known this second birth within yourself. Until then, no energy should remain dormant within you. So gather all your energies and start moving!

If you have worked hard, with determination, on the few keys I have given you, very soon you will find that a new person is being born within you, the birth of a totally new man. And the outer world will become new to the same extent as this new man has been born within you.

There is great light in the world, great brilliance and tremendous beauty, if only we have the eyes to see it and a heart to receive it. And the eyes to see and the heart to receive can be born in you. And this is the only reason that I have shared all these things with you during these last three days.

In a sense, there are not many points – in fact there are only a few. I have spoken about only two points: that life should be pure and consciousness should be empty. I have said only these two things – that life should be pure and consciousness should be empty. In fact, I have said only one thing – that consciousness should be empty. The purification of life is only a foundation for this.

When consciousness is empty, that emptiness gives you the capacity to see and unveil the hidden secret of existence. Then you don't see leaves as leaves…the life within the leaves starts becoming visible to you. And in the waves of the ocean you don't see the waves; you start seeing that which makes the waves. And then you don't see the bodies of people, you start feeling the life which is throbbing in their bodies. There is no way to describe the wonder, the miracle you start feeling.

I have invited you and called you here to move towards this mystery, and I have given you a few keys for experiencing this mystery. These keys are eternal. These keys are neither mine nor anyone else's, they are eternal. For as long as man has existed, for as long as he has had a longing for the divine, these keys have been available. They have nothing to do with any particular religion, they have nothing to do with any scriptures – they are eternal. These keys already existed before there were any scriptures or any religion, and these keys will continue to exist even if tomorrow all religious scriptures are destroyed, and all temples and mosques fall to the ground.

Religion is eternal. Sects form and disappear, religion is eternal. Scriptures are written and destroyed, religion is eternal; *tirthankaras* and *paigambaras* are born and they disappear.

It is possible that a time will come when we will forget that there was a Krishna, a Mahavira, a Christ or a Buddha – but religion will not be destroyed. Religion will not be destroyed as long as man has the thirst and quest for bliss within him, as long as man wants to rise above unhappiness.

If you are unhappy and you are aware that you are unhappy, don't go on tolerating this suffering, don't go on living with it. Stand up against the suffering and do something to get rid of it. There is very little difference between what an ordinary man does when he is in suffering and what a meditator does when he is in suffering. When an ordinary person is suffering he looks for a way to forget about it, and when a meditator is suffering he looks for a way to destroy the pain. There are only two kinds of people in the world: one kind is looking for ways to forget pain and suffering, and the other kind is looking for ways to destroy pain and suffering. I pray that you belong to the second category, not to the first one.

Trying to forget pain is a kind of unconsciousness. For twenty-four hours a day you are looking for ways to forget your pain: talking to people, listening to music, drinking alcohol, playing cards, gambling or getting involved in some other mischief where you can forget yourself, so that you forget that you have so much pain inside.

For twenty-four hours a day you are looking for ways to forget yourself. You don't want to see the pain because if you did you would be afraid. So you do all kinds of things to forget and hide the pain. But this pain will not go away by forgetting about it. This pain will no more go away by forgetting about it than wounds will heal by hiding them. Covering them with beautiful cloths does not make any difference. Instead, by covering them with beautiful cloths they will become poisonous and deadly.

So don't hide your wounds, uncover them and face your pain. And don't try to forget about it – uncover it and know it, and discover ways to destroy it. Only people who actively try to destroy the pain and not forget about it will be able to know the mystery of life.

I said that there are only two kinds of people. I call the people who are looking for a way to destroy the pain, religious. And I call the people who are looking for ways to forget the pain, irreligious. Just look at what you are doing: are you looking for ways to forget the pain? If all the ways that you try to forget pain were taken away from you, you would become even more miserable.

Once it happened to a king that one of his ministers said to him, "If we lock a man up in isolation, he will go mad within three months."

The king said, "Why should he go mad if we give him good food and good clothes?"

The minister said, "But he will go mad. Why? – because in that loneliness he will not be able to forget his pain."

So the king said, "We will see. Take the healthiest, the youngest and the happiest man in the village prisoner."

There was a young man in the village who was famous for his beauty and health. This young man was taken prisoner and locked into a cell. He was given all kinds of comforts and conveniences, good food and good clothes, but he was not given anything to pass the time. All he had were the walls and the empty room. And the guards who were put there neither understood nor spoke his language. Food was given to him, water was given to him, but he was locked up. For a day or two he really screamed about why he had been locked up, he made a big fuss. For a couple of days he did not eat. But slowly, slowly he stopped screaming and began to eat. After five to seven days it was observed that in his loneliness he was sitting and talking to himself. The minister showed him to the king through the windows: "Do you see, now he is trying the last resort to forget: he is talking to himself."

When there is nobody near you, you start talking to yourself. People often start talking to themselves as they become older. While they are young their lips are closed, but as they start growing older it is as if their lips become animated – they start talking to themselves. You must have seen people walking along the road talking to themselves. What are they doing? – they are trying to forget themselves.

For three months this young man remained locked up. When he was released after three months he had gone mad. What does it mean that he had gone mad? It means that he had created an imaginary world around himself: he had friends and enemies, he fought with them and talked with them. What does his madness imply? – it implies that the real world was not available to him, there was no one to fight with and no one to talk to, so he created an imaginary world around himself. And then he no longer had anything to do with the real world – he had created a world of his own where he could forget himself.

This young man went mad. Any one of you would go mad if you did not have to go to the shops or to work, if you did not have to fight with people in the morning and if right after getting up in the morning you could not escape in stupidities and engage in useless activities. If you didn't have any distraction for twenty-four hours a day and you were left completely alone, then you would go mad. It is because of all these distractions that you cannot see the pain within you. If you were able to see all of this pain you would commit suicide, or you would find a way to go mad by using your imagination to forget yourself.

A religious person is someone who, if left alone, utterly alone, will feel neither pain nor look for an escape.

In Germany there was once a monk named Eckhart. One day he had gone to the forest and was sitting alone under a tree. Some of his friends were also walking in the forest. When they saw that Eckhart was alone they went to him and said, "Friend, we saw that you were sitting here alone, so we thought we would come and keep you company."

Eckhart looked at them and said, "Friends, until now I was with God. Your arrival has made me feel lonely."

What he said is truly amazing! You are just the opposite: You are with someone or other for twenty-four hours a day so that you don't have to be with yourself. You are with someone or other for twenty-four hours a day so that you don't encounter yourselves. You are afraid of yourself; in this world everybody is afraid of himself. This fear of yourself is a dangerous thing.

The keys that I have mentioned will introduce you to yourself and destroy this fear, and you will be in a state where even if you were completely alone on this planet, totally alone, you would be just as blissful as if the whole earth were full of people. You will be in the same bliss totally alone as you would be with people around you. Only someone who has experienced the bliss of being alone will not be afraid of death – because death makes you completely alone. What else can it do? The only reason why you are so afraid of death is that you have never existed, only the crowd has existed. But death will take away the crowd; it will take away all your relationships and you will be left all alone – and loneliness brings fear.

All that we have discussed about meditation during these three days is basically an experiment in becoming totally alone, of moving into total aloneness. You have to go to the center where only you are and nobody else.

And this center is incredible. Someone who experiences this center will experience the depths that are beneath the ocean. You are only floating on the waves of the ocean, and you are unaware that beneath these waves are hidden infinite depths where no wave has ever gone, where no wave has ever entered.

There are many depths within you. In aloneness, the more you walk away from people and into yourself, the more you drop others and walk within yourself, the deeper you will enter into yourself. And it is a great mystery that the deeper you go within yourself, the more heights you achieve in your outer life.

It is a mathematical principle. It is a principle of the mathematics of life that the deeper you go within yourself the more height you will experience in your outer life, and the less deep you go within yourself, the fewer the heights on the outside. Someone who has not gone deeply into himself at all will have no heights on the outside. We call those people great who have depth within themselves, and as a result of this depth also have height on the outside.

So if you want height in your life you will have to go deep within yourself. The source of your depth is *samadhi*. Samadhi is the ultimate depth.

I have said a few things to you about how to take steps towards samadhi: how to discipline yourself and take care of yourself, and how to sow the seeds which will grow into divine flowers. But if even just a few things stick to your mind, if even one seed falls into the soil of your heart, there is no reason why it should not sprout and give you the experience of a new life.

Drop the desire to go on living your life in the same way as you have been living it. There is no meaning in it. Make space in your life for something new. If you go on living in the same way that you have been living, death will be the only outcome.

This desire, this discontent must come alive in you. I have no other wish for you than this. Usually people say that religion is contentment. And I say that only religious people become discontented. Everything in life only creates discontent in them, and only then do they begin to look towards religion.

So I don't ask you to be contented. I don't ask you to be satisfied. I ask you to be dissatisfied, to be utterly dissatisfied. Let every cell of your heart, of your soul be discontented – discontented for the divine, discontented for truth. In the fire of this discontent you will have a new birth.

Don't waste even a moment for this new birth. Don't make time an obstacle to it. And for this new birth, also keep in mind...

Someone was asking me yesterday: *Do we need to re-nounce the world for this kind of meditation? Will we need to become sannyasins? What will happen to our families, to our world when we practice this emptiness?*

It is important that I should say something to you on this last day about this. I tell you, religion is not against the family and the world, religion is not opposed to the family and the world. And this idea which has taken root in your mind over the past decades and centuries has harmed both you and religion very much.

Religion is not against the world. Religion is not against the family. Religion has nothing to do with dropping everything and running away. Religion is a transformation of your consciousness. It has nothing to do with outer circumstances, it has to do with the state of your mind. It is a matter of changing your mind, not your circumstances. You change yourself.

Nobody is transformed by running away from the outer world. If I am filled with hatred, what will I do in the forest? – I will also be full of hatred there. If I am full of ego, what will I do in the mountains? – I will still be full of ego, plus there will be another danger. As long as I lived in the society, in the crowd, I would come across my ego every day. But in the coolness of the Himalayas, sitting on a mountain, there will not be any people and I will not notice my own ego. And not to notice it is a totally different thing from the ego disappearing.

I have heard about a *sadhu* who was in the Himalayas for thirty years, and he felt that in those thirty years he had become totally silent and that his ego had disappeared. Then some of his disciples said to him, "There is a religious fair in the valley, and we would like you to come to it."

So they went down for the fair. But when they entered the crowd and a stranger stepped on the sadhu's foot, he immediately realized that his anger and his ego had been aroused again. He was very surprised: "A stranger stepping on my foot has shown me what the Himalayas could not show me in thirty years."

So there is no point in escaping. You don't have to escape, you have to transform. So don't take escaping as a key to life, but rather take transformation as the key. When religion became based on escapism it became lifeless. When religion again becomes based on transformation it will regain its life-energy. Remember, you have to change yourself, not your environment.

It is meaningless to change your environment. It is deceptive to change your environment because by doing this you may not notice certain things. In a new environment, in a new, silent atmosphere you may start thinking that you have become silent.

A silence which does not survive in unfavorable circumstances is not silence at all. This is why the people who are intelligent choose to practice their silence in unfavorable circumstances, because if they attain it in these unfavorable circumstances then this is the real silence.

This is why it is not a matter of running away from life. Take life as a test. And remember that all the people around you are helpful to you. The man who abused you in the morning is also helping you; he has given you an opportunity. If you want to, you can find love within yourself. Someone who expresses their anger towards you is helping you, someone who criticizes you is helping you. A man who spatters mud all over you is helping you. Someone who spreads thorns on your path is also helping you, because that is also an opportunity and a test. If you are able to go beyond it, you will feel indebted to him. What the saints cannot teach you in this world, your enemies can.

I will say it again: what saints cannot teach you in this world, enemies can. If you are alert and have the intelligence to learn, you can make a ladder out of each and every stone in your life. But the ignorant people take even stepping-stones to be obstacles and stop there. If you are intelligent, then every stone can be made a stepping-stone. If you are intelligent, every stone can be a step.

Think about this a little. Make your house, your family and all the things which seem like obstacles to you – because you think that they can prevent you from becoming silent – the center of your meditation, and you will see that those very things will help you to be silent. What are the things that don't allow you to be silent? What is the obstacle in the family? What are the things that prevent you? Just think about whether there might be a way to make them into stepping-stones. There definitely are ways. And if you think about it and understand it, you will find a way.

What is the logic that tells you that if you drop the family you will become silent and experience truth? There is no real logic. Try to understand your life and your mind rightly, and use all the circumstances around you. But what do you do? You don't use these circumstances, instead the circumstances use you. You remain lost your whole life because you don't make use of the circumstances and instead allow them to make use of you. And you remain lost because you go on reacting, you never act.

If you insult me, I will immediately insult you even more strongly. If you abuse me I will abuse you, even more so, using even more abusive words. And I will not think that I have just reacted. One abusive word has been said to me, so I return two. This is not an action, it is reaction.

If you look at your life for twenty-four hours, you will find that there are only reactions. Somebody does something, and in reaction to that you do something. I ask you, do you do anything which is not a reaction to something else, which is not a reply to something, which has not come as a reaction to something, which is not a reaction but an action? This is the discipline of action.

If you think about it, you will see that you are reacting twenty-four hours a day. Others do something, and you do something in reaction to that. Have you ever done anything which only you have done, something which originated in you and took birth in you? Just look at it and meditate on it...so that right in the middle of the family, the house and the world, you attain *sannyas*.

Sannyas is not in opposition to the world; sannyas is a purification of the world. If you start becoming pure within the world, one day you will find that you have become a sannyasin. To be a sannyasin is not a change of clothing... that you change your clothes and you become a sannyasin. Sannyas is the transformation, the development of your total being. Sannyas is a growth. It is a slow, very slow development.

If a person uses his life rightly, using whatever circumstances arise, he will find that slowly, slowly a sannyasin is taking birth within him. It is a matter of thinking about your attitudes and making them pure and empty.

Look within yourself and see what attitudes you have that are making you worldly. Remember, other people are not making you worldly. You are with your family...now how can your father or your wife make you worldly? It is the feelings of attachment that you have for your father or your wife that make you worldly.

What will happen if you escape from your wife? – those attachments will go with you. Nobody can run away from their attachments. If we were able to run away from them, life would be very easy. But if you run, all your attachments will go with you just as your shadow follows you – you will impose them on something else; you will create a new household somewhere else.

Even your so-called great sannyasins end up creating large households. They have their household, and new attachments, new infatuations arise; and again they start living between happiness and sorrow. Because they bring these attachments with them, they will come up in a new place also. It doesn't make any difference. People may change but these things will remain the same.

So I don't tell you to drop things and run away. I tell you to drop the attitudes. Things will remain as they are, but your attitudes towards them will change – and you will be free.

There was once a king in Japan. A sannyasin had lived outside this king's village for some time, lying under a tree. He was a unique sannyasin: he had much grace and radiance, much light – there was so much fragrance in his life! Gradually, as the king became attracted by this magnetism he went to him. He watched him lying there for many days, and often went to sit at his feet. The sannyasin's influence grew on the king, and one day he said to him, "Wouldn't it be better if you left this tree and came with me to the palace?"

The sannyasin said, "As you like. I can go anywhere."

The king was a little surprised. The respect he had been feeling for all those days received a shock. He had thought the sannyasin would say, "Palace? But I am a sannyasin. What would I do in a palace?"

This is what sannyasins usually say if their sannyas is a learned thing: their answer will be, "We sannyasins have nothing to do with palaces; we have dropped them." But this sannyasin said, "As you like. I can go anywhere."

The king was shocked. And he thought, "What kind of a sannyasin is this?"

But he had given the invitation himself, so he could not take it back. He had to take him. So the sannyasin went with the king who made all the necessary arrangements for him, just as he would for himself. The sannyasin started living there and enjoying himself. Big beds were made for him, and he slept in them. Big carpets were spread for him, and he walked on them. Delicious food was given to him, and he ate it. The king was no longer doubtful, he was sure. He felt, "What kind of a sannyasin is this? He has not said even once that he would not be able to sleep on those mattresses, that he could only sleep on boards. He did not say even once that he would not be able to eat such delicious food, that he could only eat very simple food."

It became more and more difficult for the king to deal with his living there. Only a week or ten days had passed when the king said to him, "Excuse me, but I have a doubt in my mind."

And the sannyasin said, "It is not only now, it was already there on the day you asked me to come with you. This doubt did not start just now, it already started on that day. But tell me, what is the doubt?"

And the king told him, "The doubt is about what kind of a sannyasin you are, and what the difference is between you, a sannyasin, and me, a worldly man?"

The sannyasin said, "If you want to see the difference come with me outside the village."

The king said, "I want to know. My mind is very disturbed by this doubt. Now even my sleep is disturbed. It was better when you were under the tree, then I had respect for you. Now that you are in the palace my respect is gone."

The sannyasin then took the king outside the village area. When they had crossed the river that was the boundary of the village, they continued to walk. So the king said, "Please tell me now."

But the sannyasin said, "Let's walk a little further."

It became very hot. It was midday and the sun was overhead. The king said, "At least tell me now. We have come very far."

The sannyasin said, "This is what I want to say: that now I will not return, I will keep on walking. Are you coming with me?"

Then the king said, "How can I come with you? I have left my family, my wife and my kingdom behind."

But the sannyasin told him, "If you are able to see the difference, see it. I'm going on, and I have left nothing behind. When I was in the palace, I was in the palace but the palace was not within me. I was inside the palace but the palace was not inside me. That is why I can go now."

The king fell at his feet. His doubt was cleared. He said, "Forgive me! I will repent all my life. Please return."

The sannyasin said, "I can still return, but your doubt will also return. It does not matter to me if I return instead of going on. I can – but your doubt will again return. Out of compassion for you I will keep on going."

The words he said are worth remembering. He said, "Out of compassion for you now I will keep on going. My compassion tells me to go on."

And I remind you that Mahavira's nakedness is more out of his compassion for you than out of any compulsion to be naked. And a true sannyasin lying in the forest? – it is less because of his attachment to lying in the forest than out of compassion for you. And going naked from door to door to ask for alms is less because of a desire to beg than out of compassion for you. Otherwise, instead of begging he could be living in your house, and instead of sleeping outside on the road he could be sleeping in a palace.

It makes no difference to a sannyasin. Yes, it does make a difference to a pseudo-sannyasin.

It does not make any difference to a true sannyasin because nothing enters his consciousness. Things are in their own place; the walls of the palace are where they are; the cushions that we are sitting on are in their place. If they don't enter my consciousness then I am untouched by them; I am far away from them.

I don't ask you to leave wherever you are. I only ask you to change what you are. I don't ask you to escape from where you are; weak people escape. I ask you to change, and this change is the real thing.

Become aware of the state of your mind and start trying to change it. Take any one aspect and start working from there. Drop by drop the ocean can become full. Walking, inch by inch, the divine can be found. Just take one step at a time. I'm not asking you to do more than that. The divine can be found simply by taking one step at a time. And don't think that you don't have the capacity, that you will not be able to attain.

Somebody was saying to me, "I am weak, I don't have much capacity. How am I to attain?"

However weak you are, everyone is capable of taking one step. And do I need to ask you…have even the most capable people ever taken more than one step at a time? Even the most capable have not taken more than one step at a time. And everyone is able to take one step at a time.

So take a step. And then take another step. You always

have to take only one step. But someone who keeps on taking only one step at a time will cover infinite distances. And anyone who does not take a step because he thinks nothing much can happen by taking one step at a time will never reach anywhere.

So I invite you to take that one step. You have listened to my talks with so much love and with so much patience. I feel a great joy and gratitude for that. I am grateful to you. I am very grateful for the place you have given me in your hearts. For this, please accept my many, many thanks and my love.

Now we will sit for today's last meditation experiment, and then we will say goodbye and leave. And I say goodbye to you with this hope: that when we meet again, I will find your silence has deepened and your bliss has grown; that you will have taken the step that I have asked you to take; that a few drops of the nectar will have entered you and that you will have come closer to deathlessness. May the divine give you the capacity to at least take one step. After that, the next steps will happen by themselves.

After the night meditation we will leave silently. In the morning I may not be able to see you as I will leave at five o'-clock. So take this as my last farewell.

Each and every person please accept my greeting to the divine that dwells within you. Please accept my greetings.

ABOUT OSHO

*O*SHO was born in Kuchwada, Madhya Pradesh, India, on December 11, 1931. From his earliest childhood, his was a rebellious and independent spirit, insisting on experiencing the truth for himself rather than acquiring knowledge and beliefs given by others.

After his enlightenment at the age of twenty-one, Osho

completed his academic studies and spent several years teaching philosophy at the University of Jabalpur. Meanwhile, he traveled throughout India giving talks, challenging orthodox religious leaders in public debate, questioning traditional beliefs, and meeting people from all walks of life. He read extensively, everything he could find to broaden his understanding of the belief systems and psychology of contemporary man.

By the late 1960s Osho had begun to develop his unique Dynamic Meditation techniques. Modern man, he says, is so burdened with the outmoded traditions of the past and the anxieties of modern-day living that he must go through a deep cleansing process before he can hope to discover the thought-less, relaxed state of meditation.

In the course of his work, Osho has spoken on virtually every aspect of the development of human consciousness. He has distilled the essence of what is significant to the spiritual quest of contemporary man, based not on intellectual understanding but tested against his own existential experience.

He belongs to no tradition – "I am the beginning of a totally new religious consciousness," he says. "Please don't connect me with the past – it is not even worth remembering."

His talks to disciples and seekers from all over the world have been published in more than six hundred and fifty volumes, and translated into over forty languages. And he says, "My message is not a doctrine, not a philosophy. My message is a certain alchemy, a science of transformation, so only those who are willing to die as they are and be born again into something so new that they cannot even imagine it right now...only those few courageous people will be ready to listen, because listening is going to be risky.

"Listening, you have taken the first step towards being re-born. So it is not a philosophy that you can just make an overcoat of and go bragging about. It is not a doctrine where you can find consolation for harassing questions. No, my message is not some verbal communication. It is far more risky. It is nothing less than death and rebirth."

Osho left his body on January 19, 1990. His huge commune in India, Osho Commune International, continues to be the largest spiritual growth center in the world attracting thousands of international visitors who come to participate in its meditation, therapy, bodywork and creative programs, or just to experience being in a buddhafield.

Osho Commune International

The Osho Commune International in Pune, India, guided by the vision of the enlightened master Osho, might be described as a laboratory, an experiment in creating a 'new man' – a human being who lives in harmony with himself and his environment, and who is free from all ideologies and belief systems which now divide humanity.

The Osho Commune's Multiversity is the biggest and most comprehensive center for personal growth in the world today. It offers a wide variety of meditation and growth awareness programs, many of which are specifically designed for newcomers.

The eight faculties of the Multiversity cover all the healing arts of East and West, most of the Western therapy approaches, the esoteric sciences, martial arts, creative arts and Zen sports, a meditation academy and numerous trainings in many of these approaches.

All these programs are designed to help people to discover the knack of meditation: the passive witnessing of thoughts, emotions and actions, without judgment or identification.

Unlike the many traditional Eastern disciplines, meditation at Osho Commune is an inseparable part of everyday life – working, relating or just being. The result is that people do not renounce the world but bring to it a spirit of awareness and celebration, in a deep reverence for life.

The highlight of the day at the Commune is the Meeting of the Osho White Robe Brotherhood. This two-hour celebration of music, dance and silence, followed by a discourse from Osho, is unique – a complete meditation in itself where thousands of seekers, in Osho's words, "dissolve into a sea of consciousness."

Further Reading

TANTRA, THE SUPREME UNDERSTANDING
Talks on the Tantric way of Tilopa's song of Mahamudra

Nothing much is known about the Indian master Tilopa, yet his mystical insight into Tantra in the form of a song passed on to his disciple Naropa, has lived on through the ages. In this series of discourses Osho speaks on Tilopa's verses, which contain many significant meditation techniques.   ISBN 81 7261 009 2

MEDITATION: THE ART OF ECSTASY

Emphasizing the "festive dimension" of meditation, Osho suggests a variety of techniques specially designed for today's Western seeker. He also provides detailed descriptions of each stage of Dynamic Meditation.   ISBN 81 7261 000 9

AND THE FLOWERS SHOWERED
Talks on Zen

Commenting on eleven Zen anecdotes, Osho explores the spiritual search – speaking on emptiness and no-mind, knowledge and being; on belief and trust, repression and truth; on philosophy and religion, love and divinity; on death and disease, on happiness and living in the here-and-now.   ISBN 81 7261 002 5

SEEDS OF WISDOM

Seeds of Wisdom is a collection of 120 letters written by Osho to a beloved disciple. The selections in this book are actually more like small stories and parables than letters. Using incidents in his daily life as a starting point, or recalling ancient teaching stories, Osho reflects on the nature of truth and the spiritual search, while at the same time giving the reader an intimate glimpse into his own life and search.   ISBN 81 7261 018 1

Further Information

To place an order or to make an inquiry, please contact:

Osho Commune International
17 Koregaon Park
Pune 411 001, MS, India
Tel: +91 (0) 212 628 562
Fax: +91 (0) 212 624 181
e-mail: osho-commune@osho.org

Osho International
570 Lexington Avenue
New York, NY 10022
Tel: +1 212 588 9888
Fax: +1 212 588 1977
e-mail:osho_int@osho.org
Web:www.osho.org

Internet
http://www.osho.org
on-line book catalog, information about Osho,
Osho's meditation techniques,
worldwide contact addresses and information.